WORKBOOK
to quench your thirst for more tools, tips and templates from

Mastering the Management Buckets
20 Critical Competencies for Leading Your Business or Nonprofit
by John Pearson

ManagementBuckets.com

a PEARPOD resource

SECOND EDITION ◆ **JULY 2018** ◆ **17% FEWER TYPOS!**

Mastering the Management Buckets Workbook

Order additional copies at Amazon.com

A RESOURCE FROM:

PEARPOD.com

For more information:

JOHN PEARSON ASSOCIATES, INC.
Board Governance & Management Consultants
P.O. Box 74985
San Clemente, CA 92673
Office: (949) 500-0334
info@JohnPearsonAssociates.com
ManagementBuckets.com

PEARPOD
Jason Pearson
San Clemente, California
Office: 949.212.7681
info@pearpod.com

Unless otherwise indicated, all Scripture quotations are taken from THE MESSAGE. Copyright © by Eugene H. Peterson 1993, 1994, 1995, 1996, 2000, 2001, 2002. Used by permission of Tyndale House Publishers, Inc.

The book reviews and links to book reviews are from *Your Weekly Staff Meeting* eNewsletter, published and edited by John Pearson. For a complimentary eNews subscription, visit:

ManagementBuckets.com/eNews

Reviews of many of the books mentioned can be located online by searching [book title, John Pearson's Buckets Blog]. Archives of the reviews are posted at:

urgentink.typepad.com

This workbook is a complementary resource to the book:

Mastering the Management Buckets: 20 Critical Competencies for Leading Your Business or Nonprofit, by John Pearson, published by Regal Books, 2008. The book and ebook are now distributed by Baker Publishing Group at BakerPublishingGroup.com and the book is also available on Amazon:

http://amzn.to/2xb872A

Printed in the USA by CreateSpace, an Amazon Company. ISBN (see back cover)

Mastering the Management Buckets
The 20 Critical Competencies

Appreciation for
Mastering the Management Buckets

☑ **BLOCKING AND TACKLING.** As John mentions in his book, I served 27 years as a Chamber of Commerce president—and worked with 27 different board chairs! I learned early on that it took a committed team of board members, staff and volunteers to achieve our mission. Leadership and management can be complex—but it's mostly about the basics: blocking and tackling. This book will bring you back to the basics. I recommend it!

GEORGE DUFF, *Former President*
Greater Seattle Chamber of Commerce, and Senior Adviser, Christian Management Association

☑ **SUPREMELY USEFUL.** This is certainly one of the first books a Christian leader should read. John puts the cookies on the lowest shelf. He speaks from the perspective of 30 years as a CEO, the perspective you have as a Christian leader. Yea God! Yea John! This is a very practical, supremely useful book. It deserves a wide audience.

BOB BUFORD (1939-2018), *Chairman of the Board*
The Buford Foundation & Leadership Network

☑ **SUPPORTS OUR MISSION.** ECFA is an accreditation agency dedicated to helping Christian ministries earn the public's trust through adherence to *Seven Standards of Responsible Stewardship*™, which focus on board governance, financial transparency, integrity in fundraising, and proper use of charity resources. *Mastering the Management Buckets* is a helpful resource that supports the mission of ECFA.

DAN BUSBY, *President*
ECFA

☑ **HARVARD MBA.** *Mastering the Management Buckets* is simply the best book I have read on Christian management of nonprofit organizations. It is a perfect balance between Biblical wisdom and a Harvard MBA.

DENNIS BAKKE
Author of the national best-selling book, *Joy at Work*

☑ **BITE-SIZED.** In *Mastering the Management Buckets*, John Pearson provides practical advice in an easily consumable format. It's bite-sized and offers easy to use job aids, charts, examples and tools to process what he's challenging us to do. This management handbook is a must read!

WENDY SEIDMAN, *Former Executive Director of Content Development and Training,* Willow Creek Association; now *President/Chief Learning Officer,* GotInfluence?

☑ **BETTER LEADER.** Reading this book and acting on its advice will make you a better leader and manager. I couldn't be more clear about that!

SANTIAGO "JIMMY" MELLADO, *Former President,* Willow Creek Association; *now President and CEO,* Compassion International

☑ **COMPASS.** Recently with the purchase of your book, *Mastering the Management Buckets*, our general manager and I are going through it purposefully, chapter by chapter, taking it apart and spending time seeing how we can look at what we doing, how we can serve our customers better and maintain a strong forging ahead momentum that hits the target of need, not the target of perceived need. So we are on an exciting journey here with the book as a compass, making sure we are headed in the "right direction."

GRAEME PARIS, *Former Executive Director*
Willow Creek Association UK & Ireland

☑ **UNDER YOUR PILLOW!** *Mastering the Management Buckets* is like a bible for managers. We all have tools we go to again and again to get the job done and John Pearson has given us that kind of tool. Put this book on your desk, not on your book shelf. If you are just getting into the management business you may want to sleep with it under your pillow! The buckets and balls arrangement of the book help you find bottom line answers for those tough management challenges right when you need them. While the book is built on a foundation of sound management theories, each chapter (bucket) leads you into the personal action next steps required of a wise, skillful and competent leader.

GARY BISHOP (1946-2015)
President, Far Corners Mission

☑ **FRESH REMINDER.** As World Vision helps transform the lives of the world's poorest children and families in nearly 100 countries, we strive to be leaders and managers who honor God every day. That's not easy! *Mastering the Management Buckets* is a fresh reminder of the complexity of the leadership challenge—yet John's book also delivers practical management insights for our leaders and our in-the-trenches people.

RICHARD E. STEARNS, *President*
World Vision U.S.

☑ **TAKE NOTES!** John Pearson has written a wonderful book that is not only for those aspiring to leadership positions, but those who have been in the management ranks for years. I not only enjoyed it, I learned a few things to boot! So buy the book, grab a cup of coffee, put your feet up, and take notes!

DIANE PASSNO, *Former Senior Vice President*
Focus on the Family

Introduction

**"...leadership is a complex field and no one resource
can meet all the needs of every leader in every situation."**
Richard Kriegbaum[1]

So...What's With the Buckets and the Balls
in Mastering the Management Buckets?

I was unprepared for leadership. I didn't know what I didn't know. But over the years, patient bosses, boards and mentors guided me in my life-long learning leadership and management journey. *I'm still learning.*

So the book—and this Workbook—is a crash course in Leadership and Management 101. It's more pragmatic than comprehensive. It's part resource library, part filing system and part tool box.

Somewhere along the journey I created my 20 management buckets system. I observed leaders and managers who excelled in The Customer Bucket, but didn't know what they didn't know in The People Bucket. Not all buckets are created equal, but to be effective, you must know the 20 buckets and the critical balls in each bucket. This book is just an introduction to Buckets 101. It won't solve all your management challenges. No book will.

In my camp director days, I'd marvel at the people skills of creative program directors, but wince at their inability to energize the team at the weekly staff meeting. They had most of the core competencies in The Program Bucket, but were unaware of the critical balls in The Meetings Bucket. So, the Law of Unintended Consequences frequently derailed thoughtful programs, products and services. Good ideas. Poor execution.

Some managers bring three baseball caps to their staff meetings labeled: CAUSE, COMMUNITY and CORPORATION. The buckets are organized under these three arenas and it's vital that when you speak, your team members know which hat you're wearing.

The CAUSE is all about your mission, your customer, your strategy, your programs, products and services—and the results you are targeting. The language of CAUSE is purpose-driven, energetic, and many times laced with athletic and military imagery. "OK, team, let's get out there and take that hill. Win one for the Gipper!"

The buckets in the COMMUNITY arena are no less important, but the vocabulary is softer. Here we hone our core competencies in people skills and we seek to create a God-honoring culture with three to five core values. In the COMMUNITY, we build and equip team members and we celebrate results using tools from The *Hoopla!* Bucket. We invest time in affirmation—not because it increases revenue, but because it honors our people.

---

[1] R. Scott Rodin, *Steward Leader Meditations: Fifty Devotions for the Leadership Journey* (Colton, WA: Kingdom Life Publishing, 2016), 13

Leaders of nonprofit organizations and churches, who work with donors and volunteers, will balance the CAUSE rhetoric with the warm language of COMMUNITY. "We are extraordinarily blessed by our volunteers."

When a leader or manager wears the CORPORATION hat, the focus is on operations, systems, marketing and public relations, boards and meetings. Here managers focus on their fiduciary responsibilities, hiring and firing employees, delegation, organizational charts and budgets—not the stuff of the touchy feely COMMUNITY arena nor the compelling vision of the CAUSE —but no less important. *It takes a village of buckets and balls to build a sustainable company or organization.*

Each "bucket" represents a core competency that every effective organization must master. At the beginning of each chapter (in the book and in this workbook), you'll find the core competency—the "bucket"—that will be fleshed out with insights and assignments.

Within each bucket, there are two to six "balls"—which represent the specific action steps needed to excel at that competency. Every "ball" is a verb—think action, execution, and implementation. This system is not dry theory—it's in the trenches, real-life stuff.

> **No one person can master the core competencies in all 20 management buckets.**

When you use the "buckets" and "balls" language with your team members, you will help them see the big picture: how each person's work contributes to your organization's mission.

The 20 management buckets have worked well for me, but you may want to use different labels for your "buckets" and "balls." The point is to perfect a leadership and management philosophy and system and—as Peter Drucker preached—practice, practice, practice the art of management.

Enjoy drinking from the buckets!

How to Use This Workbook

❑ Option 1: Study on your own.

❑ Option 2: Study with your coach or mentor.

❑ Option 3: Study with your team members—and integrate what you're learning into your projects every week. Award Starbucks cards to those who apply what they're learning!

❑ Option 4: (create your own plan)

20 Days, 20 Months or 20 Years

There are several ways to digest the book and the workbook. After you've read it, create a buckets system for yourself. I'm partial to three-ring binders, with 20 tabs—but you may prefer 20 file folders. When you find something helpful, in the newspaper or at a workshop, drop the insight into the appropriate bucket filing system.

To move to Level 3 (I have an action plan to address what I know I don't know), consider these options:

❑ **20 Days.** Designate the next 20 working days and each day, for one hour, review one bucket (one chapter). Focus on one or two strategic next steps and add them to your To Do list.

❑ **20 Months.** Set aside one full day per month, over the next 20 months, and learn all you can about honing your core competencies within one bucket on that day and during that month.

❑ **20 Years.** If you're under 45 and one of your Top-5 strengths is "learner" (see The Team Bucket), you might enjoy focusing on one bucket a year, while cherry picking insights from the other buckets throughout the year. If you invest 20 years in 20 buckets, you'll be a world class management expert and someone will name a bucket in your honor (see The Drucker Bucket).

❑ **20 Flipchart Sheets.** My friends, Don and Ele Parrott attended my two-day *Management Buckets Workshop Experience* and then debriefed the sessions with Don's management team. At a one-day retreat, they mounted 20 flipchart sheets around the room—and using post-it notes—agreed on next steps, with deadline dates, for future projects within each bucket. That was brilliant!

Enjoy the Journey

At my two-day workshops, I share dozens of war stories from my reckless management years—before I understood the 20 buckets and before I understood holy ground. I wish I could go back and edit my life's video, but I can't. Hopefully, this book will save you some scars and scares, and also lighten your load on your God-honoring management journey.

John Pearson

Mastering the Management Buckets WORKBOOK is a resource from:

Visit the website to learn how the creative team at PEARPOD has helped hundreds of organizations make something great together.

PEARPOD.com

Unexpected Creative. More than just a slogan, it is our approach to every project. Today with more marketing channels than ever before, it is easy to get lost in the spin cycle. Pearpod collaborates with you to develop something truly original. Our services include everything from branding to print to video to the latest digital methods that will connect with your unique audience.

We love what we do. Whether it is large campaign for Mercedes-Benz or a niche fundraising opportunity for a start-up nonprofit, we are ready for the challenge. At the end of the day it's about your results and not our egos. Take a digital stroll through our website and see if anything inspires you. *Let's make something great together.*

Call or text us at 949.212.7681 or email info@Pearpod.com

☑ THE CAUSE
❑ THE COMMUNITY
❑ THE CORPORATION

Cause, Community, Corporation: The 3-legged Stool

"The CAUSE is all about our mission, our customers, our strategy, our programs, our products and our services—and it's about the results we are targeting. The language of Cause is purpose-driven, energetic and many times laced with athletic and military imagery. "OK, team…let's get out there and take that hill. Win one for the Gipper!"[2]

---

[2] John Pearson, *Mastering the Management Buckets*, 24.

THE CAUSE

THE CAUSE
Bucket 1: The Results Bucket
Bucket 2: The Customer Bucket
Bucket 3: The Strategy Bucket
Bucket 4: The Drucker Bucket
Bucket 5: The Book Bucket
Bucket 6: The Program Bucket

THE COMMUNITY
Bucket 7: The People Bucket
Bucket 8: The Culture Bucket
Bucket 9: The Team Bucket
Bucket 10: The *Hoopla!* Bucket
Bucket 11: The Donor Bucket
Bucket 12: The Volunteer Bucket
Bucket 13: The Crisis Bucket

THE CORPORATION
Bucket 14: The Board Bucket
Bucket 15: The Budget Bucket
Bucket 16: The Delegation Bucket
Bucket 17: The Operations Bucket
Bucket 18: The Systems Bucket
Bucket 19: The Printing Bucket
Bucket 20: The Meetings Bucket

#1: THE RESULTS BUCKET

FOCUS ON S.M.A.R.T. GOALS:

Board members frequently note that staff reports at board meetings are filled with activity, but rarely is the activity linked to agreed-upon S.M.A.R.T. goals. As Fred Smith, Sr. reminds us:

"Many regale others (especially bosses) with the details of exhausting activity: how many miles they traveled, how tough the job is, how many hours they worked, etc. expecting this to make up for lack of activity. It is my experience that those who use activity to produce results downplay the preparation and highlight the outcome. Reports of poor production are often prefaced with excuses and rationalizations.

"One of my more caustic friends was listening to a young executive tell how tired he was. The young employee went through how much trouble he had on the job, how difficult it was, and what unexpected problems arose. In the midst of this my friend interrupted, **'Please show me the baby and don't tell me about the labor pains.'**

"I totally grabbed that and my children, business associates, and others who come for counsel will hear it if they start wandering down the activity trail instead of showing results."[3]

---

[3] Fred Smith, Sr. "Be Ye Doers," from the August 22, 2017 *Weekly Thought* website, "Breakfast With Fred: Timeless Wisdom for Today's Leaders" - http://www.breakfastwithfred.com/weeklythought/1721/

1. THE RESULTS BUCKET

CORE COMPETENCY

> **"We focus on results.** We are not activity-driven, we are results-driven. We measure what we value, so we celebrate both the writing and the achieving of team-blessed standards of performance for every staff member, board member and volunteer. We also abandon dead horses and sacred cows."

Strategic Balls in the Results Bucket

❶ MANAGE for results.

❷ FOCUS on outside results, not inside results.

❸ PRIORITIZE results with S.M.A.R.T. standards of performance (SMART Goals).

❹ MEASURE your results.

❺ SLOUGH OFF yesterday.

SELF-ASSESSMENT:

☑ **Where is your ORGANIZATION or DEPT. today? What's your 1-year goal?**

	4 LEVELS OF MANAGEMENT KNOWLEDGE AND COMPETENCIES	**TODAY**	**IN 1 YEAR:**
Level 1	I don't know what I don't know.		
Level 2	I know what I don't know.		
Level 3	I have an action plan to address what I know I don't know.		
Level 4	I am knowledgeable and effective in this core competency and can mentor others.		

☑ **Where are YOU today? What's your 1-year goal?**

	4 LEVELS OF MANAGEMENT KNOWLEDGE AND COMPETENCIES	**TODAY**	**IN 1 YEAR:**
Level 1	I don't know what I don't know.		
Level 2	I know what I don't know.		
Level 3	I have an action plan to address what I know I don't know.		
Level 4	I am knowledgeable and effective in this core competency and can mentor others.		

Manage for Results

Allocate resources to results—not problems.

Peter Drucker challenged nonprofit organizations and churches to focus on the "Five Most Important Questions Every Nonprofit Organization Must Ask." They are:

1) What is our mission?

2) Who is our customer?

3) What does the customer value?

4) What are our results?

5) What is our plan?

Question 4: What Are Our Results?

Adam Braun's "Millennial Takeaway" notes: "At one point a few years ago when we had built just a few schools, I wrote in my journal that if Pencils of Promise built 30 schools by the time I turned 30, I could die a happy man. Today we've opened more than 150. But here's the important part—I was wrong about being able to die a happy man. I still want to do so much more. As soon as something becomes possible, you start thinking of what you can do next."[4]

RESORCES:
❑ **The Results Bucket: www.managementbuckets.com/results-bucket**
❑ *Peter Drucker's Five Most Important Questions: Enduring Wisdom for Today's Leaders,* by Peter F. Drucker, Frances Hesselbein, and Joan Snyder Kuhl
❑ See other books by Peter Drucker (and about Drucker) in The Drucker Bucket at www.managementbuckets.com/drucker-bucket

TO DO OR TO DELEGATE:

Point Person	Task	Deadline	Done!

Bucket Bottom Line:
Are your board reports, water cooler conversations, donor letters, and your elevator speech about "activities and anecdotes" or RESULTS?

---

[4] Peter F. Drucker, Frances Hesselbein, and Joan Snyder Kuhl, *Peter Drucker's Five Most Important Questions: Enduring Wisdom for Today's Leaders* (John Wiley & Sons, Inc., Hoboken, NJ)

Focus on Outside Results, Not Inside Results

5 subtle signs about your priorities

Listen to Peter Drucker:[5]

- "Neither results, nor resources, exist inside the business. Both exist outside the business."
- "Results are obtained by exploiting opportunities, not by solving problems."
- "Resources, to produce results, must be allocated to opportunities, rather than to problems."

☑ **Evaluate:** Do you focus on inside or outside results when communicating in...

Your Communication Channels	Inside Results	Outside Results
1) Staff Meetings		
2) Newsletters and Donor Letters		
3) Elevator Speech (Your answer to: "How's it going?")		
4) Budget		
5) Celebrations		
On a scale of 1 to 10 (10 = outside results-focused), I'd give our organization a rating of:		

RESOURCES:

❑ *Peter Drucker's The Five Most Important Questions Self-Assessment Tool: Facilitator's Guide,* published by Frances Hesselbein Leadership Institute/Jossey-Bass
❑ *Peter Drucker's The Five Most Important Questions Self-Assessment Tool: Participant Workbook,* published by Frances Hesselbein Leadership Institute/Jossey-Bass

TO DO OR TO DELEGATE:

Point Person	Task	Deadline	Done!

Bucket Bottom Line:
Create an "Outside Results" culture with strategic tools and formal and informal celebrations. (See ideas in The *Hoopla!* Bucket.)

---

[5] Peter F. Drucker, *Managing for Results* (New York: Collins, 2006)

Prioritize Results With *S.M.A.R.T.* Standards of Performance (SMART Goals)

Create clear goals and a rigorous accountability system with celebration mileposts.

Inspire every team member to craft 3 to 5 annual Standards of Performance (SOPs) or SMART Goals. They must:
- Meet the S.M.A.R.T. criteria.
- Be reviewed and approved by peers, direct reports and each person's boss or board.
- Be part of a regular accountability/reporting process (usually with a monthly color-coded dashboard report).

S.M.A.R.T. Goals are:

Specific
Goals should specify what you want to achieve.

Measurable
Goals must be specific enough to be measured at the finish line.

Achievable
Goals must be attainable. No pie in the sky stuff here!

Realistic
Goals must also be realistic—in light of the <u>resources</u> you have allocated to the goal.

Time-related
Goals must have a specific date when the results will be achieved (Dec. 31, 2018).

RESOURCES:
- ❏ *Execution: The Discipline of Getting Things Done,* by Larry Bossidy and Ram Charan
- ❏ *The Three Signs of a Miserable Job,* by Patrick Lencioni
- ❏ You may prefer to use other words for "S.M.A.R.T." Visit www.acronymfinder.com.

TO DO OR TO DELEGATE:

Point Person	Task	Deadline	Done!

Bucket Bottom Line:
Faith-based Goals: "In his heart a man plans his course, but the Lord determines his steps." (Proverb 16:9)

Measure Your Results

Track your progress with leading indicators.

One-page Leading Indicators will revolutionize your work!
- Other names: Metrics, Dashboard, Goals, etc.
- See Standards of Performance in this bucket.
- See details in The Strategy Budget.
- Report monthly with just one-page.

Top 10 Leading Indicators: Monthly Update
Approved by Management Team on October 15

LEADING INDICATORS	Point Person	ANNUAL GOAL (12 Months)	YTD Goal (6 Months)	YTD Actual (6 Months)	YTD Difference
1) Revenue	Bob	$925,000	$500,000	$517,000	+$17,000
2) New volunteers	Dale	250	175	195	+20
3) New donors ($500 or more)	Sue	175	75	125	+50
4) Partnerships	Fred	5	1	2	+1
5) Regional reps trained and certified	Rob	25	12	10	-2
6) Website product downloads	Rob	10,000	3,500	5,500	+2,000
7)					
8)					
9)					
10)					

Notes: Melinda will compile and distribute this report by the fifth of each month and the Management Team will review it at our meeting on the second Wednesday of every month.

RESOURCES:
❑ *The Nonprofit Dashboard: A Tool for Tracking Progress,* by Lawrence M. Butler, BoardSource (BoardSource.org)
❑ *The ONE Thing: The Surprisingly Simple Truth Behind Extraordinary Results,* by Gary Keller with Jay Papasan (John Pearson's 2016 Book-of-the-Year)

TO DO OR TO DELEGATE:

Point Person	Task	Deadline	Done!

Bucket Bottom Line:
Without leading indicators, you are likely deluding yourself into believing that your results are acceptable, or even admirable! Without an objective target—how do you know? *(See also The Strategy Bucket.)*

(continued)

Define Quantitative and Qualitative Results
Use creativity in monitoring progress and achievements.

Ask yourself these key questions suggested by Peter Drucker:[6]
- How do we define results?
    - ➜ Quantitative
    - ➜ Qualitative
    - ➜ Perception
- Are we successful?
- How does our organization currently define results?
- How does our organization monitor progress and achievement?
- What results are currently being achieved?

Jim Collins says "all indicators are flawed."
"It doesn't really matter whether you can quantify your results. What matters is that you rigorously assemble evidence—quantitative or qualitative—to track your progress."

Discuss:
❑ Per Jim Collins, what does "greatness" look like for the Cleveland Orchestra?
❑ Per the article, "Ensuring Mission Impact," how do we move from strategy to results?

RESOURCES:
❑ *Good to Great and the Social Sectors: Why Business Thinking Is Not the Answer,* by Jim Collins
❑ Visit: www.JimCollins.com
❑ Article: "Ensuring Mission Impact: How to Move From Strategy to Results," by Matt Breitenberg and Art Caccese, *Christian Management Report* (Dec. 2003) – Download at www.managementbuckets.com/results-bucket

TO DO OR TO DELEGATE:

Point Person	Task	Deadline	Done!

Bucket Bottom Line:
Jim Collins: *"What matters is not finding the perfect indicator, but settling upon a consistent and intelligent method of assessing your output results and then tracking your trajectory with rigor. What do you mean by great performance? Have you established a baseline? Are you improving? If not, why not? How can you improve even faster toward your audacious goals?"*[7]

---

[6] Peter F. Drucker, *The Five Most Important Questions Self-Assessment Tool: Participant Workbook, Third Edition* (San Francisco: Jossey-Bass, 2010), 61.
[7] Jim Collins, *Good to Great and the Social Sectors: Why Business Thinking Is Not the Answer* (Boulder, CO: Jim Collins, 2005), 8.

Slough Off Yesterday

When the horse is dead, dismount!

> **More Drucker Insights.** Finally, look at Peter Drucker's critical questions—focused on results—and list some possibilities for your organization:
>
> # What must we strengthen?
>
> # What must we abandon?

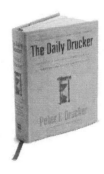

Abandonment (5 January)

"There is nothing as difficult and as expensive, but also nothing as futile, as trying to keep a corpse from stinking."

"Without systematic and purposeful abandonment, an organization will be overtaken by events. It will squander its best resources on things it should never have been doing or should no longer do. As a result, it will lack the resources, especially capable people, needed to exploit the opportunities that arise. Far too few businesses are willing to slough off yesterday, and as a result far too few have resources available for tomorrow."[8]

CONFIDENTIAL EXERCISE: "SLOUGH OFF YESTERDAY"

Trim 20% of your budget:	
Trim 20% of your staff:	

RESOURCES:

❑ Read John 15:1-2 (NIV): "I am the true vine, and my Father is the gardener. He cuts off every branch in me that bears no fruit, while every branch that does bear fruit he prunes so that it will be even more fruitful."

TO DO OR TO DELEGATE:

Point Person	Task	Deadline	Done!

Bucket Bottom Line:
Effective leaders and managers identify sacred cows and dead horses and deal with them thoughtfully and appropriately. (See the section on "social styles" in The People Bucket for clues on breaking bad news to the four styles.)

---

[8] Peter F. Drucker with Joseph A. Maciariello, *The Daily Drucker: 366 Days of Insight and Motivation for Getting the Right Things Done* (New York: HarperCollins, 2004), 7.

When the Horse Is Dead, Dismount!
Read Chapter 1: The Results Bucket (pages 35-37)

How many dead horses are you still riding, attempting to resuscitate not just a losing program or product, but a dead loser?

☑ Check the Top-5 Answers You Often Hear in Your Organization!

In the fascinating can't-put-it-down book, *Into the Future: Turning Today's Church Trends Into Tomorrow's Opportunities*, by Elmer Towns and Warren Bird, the respected authors write that "Dakota tribal wisdom says that when you discover you are riding a dead horse, the best strategy is to dismount. In contrast, here's how many in the church respond when they find out their 'horse' is dead."[9]

1. Say things like, "This is the way we always have ridden this horse."

2. Appoint a committee to study the horse.

3. Buy a stronger whip.

4. Change riders.

5. Arrange to visit other churches to see how they ride dead horses.

6. Raise the standards for riding dead horses.

7. Appoint a tiger team to revive the dead horse.

8. Create a training session to increase our riding ability.

9. Compare the state of dead horses in today's environment.

10. Change your definition or rules by declaring, "This horse is not dead."

11. Hire new staff members to ride the dead horse.

12. Harness several dead horses together for increased speed.

13. Declare that "no horse is too dead to beat."

14. Provide additional funding to increase the horse's performance.

15. Do a cost-analysis study to see if riding dead horses is cheaper.

16. Purchase a product to make dead horses run faster.

17. Declare that the horse is "better, faster, and cheaper" dead.

18. Form a quality circle to find uses for dead horses.

19. Revisit the performance requirements for horses.

20. Say this horse was procured with cost as an independent variable.

21. Promote the dead horse to a supervisory position.

---

[9] Elmer Towns and Warren Bird, *Into the Future: Turning Today's Church Trends Into Tomorrow's Opportunities* (Grand Rapids, MI: Fleming H. Revell Company, 2000), 13.

#2: THE CUSTOMER BUCKET

Jason Pearson is the author and creator of numerous projects including: *10 ADMISSIONS: Coloring Book + Ministry Storytelling Manual* (a workshop handout that morphed into a 58-page book).

COLOR COMMENTARY BY JASON PEARSON:

When inspiring our clients at PEARPOD, we drill down, ASAP, on their customer (or donor, or client, or member)—and with appreciation to Peter Drucker, we ask, **"What does your customer value?"**

We encourage clients to think about their customers using our terms for the four social styles (see The People Bucket):

TASK-ORIENTED CUSTOMERS:
❑ INFO-SPONGES:
Analytical, Logical, Loves Data

❑ JUST-THE-FACTS
Driver, Results, Efficiency

RELATIONSHIP-ORIENTED CUSTOMERS:
❑ HEARTFELT
Amiable, Supportive, Careful

❑ SHARE-MEISTER
Expressive, Enthusiastic, Unstructured

So…when designing your website, writing a donor letter, posting on social media, or preparing your annual report—does your communication tilt inappropriately to one style? **Do you communicate in refreshing and inspiring words, images, and media to all four social styles?**

2. THE CUSTOMER BUCKET

CORE COMPETENCY

> **"We know our primary and supporting customers.** We segment our customers to more effectively meet their unique needs. We listen to our customers. We are zealots for researching and understanding our markets."

Strategic Balls in the Customer Bucket

❶ FOCUS on your primary customer.

❷ IDENTIFY your supporting customers.

❸ LEARN how your customers will change.

❹ MOVE customers from ignorance to purchase.

❺ SEGMENT your customers prayerfully.

❻ RESEARCH what your customer values.

SELF-ASSESSMENT:

☑ **Where is your ORGANIZATION or DEPT. today? What's your 1-year goal?**

	4 LEVELS OF MANAGEMENT KNOWLEDGE AND COMPETENCIES	TODAY	IN 1 YEAR:
Level 1	I don't know what I don't know.		
Level 2	I know what I don't know.		
Level 3	I have an action plan to address what I know I don't know.		
Level 4	I am knowledgeable and effective in this core competency and can mentor others.		

☑ **Where are YOU today? What's your 1-year goal?**

	4 LEVELS OF MANAGEMENT KNOWLEDGE AND COMPETENCIES	TODAY	IN 1 YEAR:
Level 1	I don't know what I don't know.		
Level 2	I know what I don't know.		
Level 3	I have an action plan to address what I know I don't know.		
Level 4	I am knowledgeable and effective in this core competency and can mentor others.		

Focus on Your Primary Customer

You can't be all things to all people.

Peter Drucker challenged nonprofit organizations and churches to focus on the "Five Most Important Questions Every Nonprofit Organization Must Ask." They are:

1) What is our mission?

2) Who is our customer?

3) What does the customer value?

4) What are our results?

5) What is our plan?

Discuss: The Annual Father-Son Fishing Weekend (pages 39-40 in *Mastering the Management Buckets*)

 **"Your primary customer is the person whose life is *changed* through your work."**
Peter Drucker[10]

RESOURCES:

❑ **The Customer Bucket: www.managementbuckets.com/customer-bucket**
❑ *Duct Tape Marketing: The World's Most Practical Small Business Marketing Guide*, by John Jantsch
❑ *It's the Customer, Stupid! 34 Wake-up Calls to Help You Stay Client-Focused*, by Michael A. Aun

TO DO OR TO DELEGATE:

Point Person	Task	Deadline	Done!

Bucket Bottom Line:
God has called your unique ministry to reach and serve a primary customer. What do you know about this person and what else do you need to know?

---

[10] Peter F. Drucker, Frances Hesselbein, and Joan Snyder Kuhl, *Peter Drucker's Five Most Important Questions: Enduring Wisdom for Today's Leaders* (John Wiley & Sons, Inc., Hoboken, NJ), 20.

Identify Your Supporting Customers

To be effective: focus, focus, focus.

In the Simplified Segmenting Chart below, there are 12 groups that a church, for example, might focus on. Few churches can serve the diverse needs of all 12 groups effectively. Pray, ponder, plan and then prioritize the groups below—and concentrate your passion, your people, and your payroll on just three to five segments. *And serve them well!*

Priority #1 _____ - Our Primary Customer

Priority #2 _____ - Supporting Customers*

Priority #3 _____ - Supporting Customers*

*You may prefer to use the term "Secondary Customers." (Refer to Drucker's materials on this.)

SIMPLIFIED SEGMENTING[11] *Focus on 3 to 5 Groups*	CHILDREN	YOUTH	ADULTS
CHRISTIANS Who Attend Church	A	B	C
CHRISTIANS Who Do Not Attend Church	D	E	F
NON-CHRISTIANS Who Attend Church	G	H	I
NON-CHRISTIANS Who Do Not Attend Church	J	K	L

RESOURCES:

❑ *Marketing Your Ministry: Ten Critical Principles,* by John W. Pearson and Robert D. Hisrich, Ph.D.

❑ *The Practical Drucker: Applying the Wisdom of the World's Greatest Management Thinker,* by William A. Cohen

TO DO OR TO DELEGATE:

Point Person	Task	Deadline	Done!

Bucket Bottom Line:
You can't be all things to all people. You must identify the top three to five segments that God has called you to reach and serve. The "Go Ye" command is for the entire Body of Christ—not just your ministry!

---

[11] William Benke and Le Etta Benke, *Church Wake-Up Call: A Ministries Management Approach That Is Purpose-Oriented and Inter-Generational in Outreach* (Florence, KY: Routledge, 2001). Note: Bill Benke introduced the 12 segments concept to John Pearson in the late1970s.

Learn How Your Customers Will Change

You're serving a parade, not a crowd!

The president of the Greater Seattle Chamber of Commerce, George Duff, hung this insight on his office wall for the 27 years he served in the Emerald City:

You never get to the point where everybody
knows your story, where there is
no more criticism.
**Remember, you are talking
not to a crowd but to a parade
that is changing all the time.**

You must communicate with all the marchers.
Young people are growing up,
new people are assuming the burdens of the old,
different people are moving into your area,
even the same people
are changing their thinking.
Anonymous

Discuss: How is your customer changing? What methods will you employ to learn more about your customer?

**FEEDBACK
IS THE
BREAKFAST
OF CHAMPIONS!**[12]

RESOURCES:
❑ *Marketing Your Ministry: Ten Critical Principles,* by John W. Pearson and Robert D. Hisrich, Ph.D.
❑ *The Practical Drucker: Applying the Wisdom of the World's Greatest Management Thinker,* by William A. Cohen

TO DO OR TO DELEGATE:

Point Person	Task	Deadline	Done!

Bucket Bottom Line:
Know your customers. Some of them just changed their thinking!

---

[12] John W. Pearson and Robert D. Hisrich, Ph.D. *Marketing Your Ministry: Ten Critical Principles* (Brentwood, TN: Wolgemuth & Hyatt, Publishers, Inc., 1990). "Feedback is the breakfast of champions" is quoted often by Hisrich.

The Five Generations
Learn How Your Customers Are Different Today and How They Will Change Tomorrow

10 FACTORS:	SENIORS	BUILDERS	BOOMERS	BUSTERS	MILLENNIALS
1. Era they were born	1900-1928	1929-1945	1946-1964	1965-1983	1984-2002
2. Life paradigm	Manifest destiny	Be grateful you have a job	You owe me	Relate to me	Life is a cafeteria
3. Attitude to authority	Respect them	Endure them	Replace them	Ignore them	Choose them
4. Role of relationships	Long term	Significant	Limited: useful	Central: caring	Global
5. Value Systems	Traditional	Conservative	Self-based	Media	Shop around
6. Role of Career	Loyalty	Means for living	Central focus	Irritant	Place to serve
7. Schedules	Responsible	Mellow	Frantic	Aimless	Volatile
8. Technology	What's that?	Hope to outlive it	Master it	Enjoy it	Employ it
9. Market	Commodities	Goods	Services	Experiences	Transformations
10. View of future	Uncertain	Seek to stabilize	Create it!	Hopeless	Optimistic

Move Your Customers From Ignorance to Purchase

Use the right tools, for the right people, at the right time.

"One size fits all" is a very expensive and ineffective customer strategy. Consider your donor program. Your ministry is reaching out to new donors, thanking current donors, and wondering why your list of former donors is growing so rapidly.

Create a strategy for moving a person from "ignorance" to "purchase" (see the chart below). You'll have a different marketing and communication plan (the marketing mix) for each segment. The secret: use the right tools for the right people at the right time.

MARKETING MIX EXAMPLES:

➔ LEVEL 1: IGNORANCE. A neighbor invites a new homeowner over for coffee and mentions their involvement in a wheelchair ministry.

➔ LEVEL 2: AWARENESS. The new neighbor reads a newspaper article about the ministry and remembers the neighbor's enthusiasm.

➔ LEVEL 3: INTEREST. The neighbor's teen daughter has a new friend that sponsors a wheelchair every Christmas. "Dad, check out their website!"

➔ LEVEL 4: TRIAL OR CONSIDERATION. The family agrees to have a garage sale to raise money for wheelchairs. They give a one-time gift online.

➔ LEVEL 5: PREFERENCE. The ministry calls to thank them for the gift (within seven days) and that gets Dad's attention. "I like these folks!"

➔ LEVEL 6: PURCHASE. After attending a ministry fundraising event, the family makes a three-year major gift commitment and are volunteer zealots!

THE RIGHT TOOLS FOR THE RIGHT PEOPLE! YOUR MARKETING MIX➔	Marketing Mix Tool A Brochure	Marketing Mix Tool B Website	Marketing Mix Tool C Newsletter
1) IGNORANCE			
2) AWARENESS			
3) INTEREST			
4) TRIAL OR CONSIDERATION			
5) PREFERENCE			
6) PURCHASE			

RESOURCES:

❑ *Entrepreneurship,* by Robert D. Hisrich, Michael P. Peters and Dean A. Shepherd
❑ *The King of Madison Avenue: David Ogilvy and the Making of Modern Advertising,* by Kenneth Roman

TO DO OR TO DELEGATE:

Point Person	Task	Deadline	Done!

Bucket Bottom Line:
Target every marketing, donor and communication piece for one of the six marketing levels.

Segment Your Customers Prayerfully

Know the Engel Scale—and where your customers are today.

One size doesn't fit all—and the thoughtful preacher, teacher, evangelist, fundraiser and discipler must always communicate the Gospel in the right language to the right segment. *It takes thoughtful prayer and hard work!*

Where are students at a Young Life camp? Are they at a -8, -7, or a -4 (positive attitude toward the Gospel)? Are the men who became Christians at last year's men's retreat still at -1 or have you helped them grow to +3, +4 or +5? Don't know? You must find out—soon!

Fifty-two weeks of Sunday sermons may be 52 weeks of miscommunication if the message is targeted to +3 members, when 50 percent of the congregation is still at -1.

The Engel Scale: A Person's Response to the Gospel
Adapted from *What's Gone Wrong With the Harvest?*[13]

-8	Awareness of Supreme Being but No Effective Knowledge of Gospel
-7	Initial Awareness of Gospel
-6	Awareness of Fundamentals of Gospel
-5	Grasp of Implications of Gospel
-4	Positive Attitude Toward Gospel
-3	Personal Problem Recognition
-2	**DECISION TO ACT**
-1	Repentance and Faith in Christ

The Engel Scale: A New Christian's Growth

+1	Post-Decision Evaluation
+2	Incorporation Into Body
+3	Conceptual and Behavioral Growth
+4	Communion With God
+5	Stewardship
+6	Reproduction • Internally (gifts, etc.) • Externally (witness, social action, etc.)
↓	Etc.

RESOURCES:

❑ *What's Gone Wrong With the Harvest? A Communication Strategy for the Church and World Evangelism,* by James F. Engel & Wilbert Norton
❑ Visit: https://en.wikipedia.org/wiki/Engel_Scale

TO DO OR TO DELEGATE:

Point Person	Task	Deadline	Done!

Bucket Bottom Line:
Every Gospel communication must be targeted to a person's spiritual decision-making process and receptivity to the Gospel. (Plus, see "social styles" in The People Bucket.)

---

[13] James F. Engel & Wilbert Norton, *What's Gone Wrong With the Harvest? A Communication Strategy for The Church and World Evangelism* (Grand Rapids, MI: Zondervan Publishing House, 1975).

⑥ Research... "What does your customer value?"

Listen! Listen! Listen!

Dr. Robert D. Hisrich, the brilliant co-author of our book, *Marketing Your Ministry: 10 Critical Principles*, preaches research, research, research. He writes:

"If you have $10,000 to spend, invest $5,000 in researching and understanding the market."

"What does the customer value?" is the third question that Peter Drucker says all nonprofit organizations must ask and answer. So how do you find out what people value?

You ask, says Hisrich:

"Ask people what their real needs are, then shut up, and listen, listen, listen."

Here are several ways to research what your customers value:

- ☑ Online Surveys
- ☑ Exit Interviews
- ☑ Monthly Phone Blitz
- ☑ Annual Satisfaction Survey
- ☑ Workplace Survey

RESOURCES:

- ❑ Survey software: www.SurveyMonkey.com
- ❑ Workplace culture survey: www.bcwinstitute.com
- ❑ *Reveal: Where Are You?* by Greg L. Hawkins and Cally Parkinson (research conducted at Willow Creek Community Church)
- ❑ Visit: www.revealforchurch.com

TO DO OR TO DELEGATE:

Point Person	Task	Deadline	Done!

Bucket Bottom Line:
Maintain a "Research Wish List" and review it monthly with your management team to discern on-going and future research priorities.
- What do we need to know about our customers that we don't know today?
- Who is the point person working on this?

#3: THE STRATEGY BUCKET

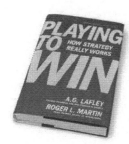

COLOR COMMENTARY BY JASON PEARSON:

Sometimes the most innocent question or request can lead to a major breakthrough!

For example, a few years ago, a client asked for a website refresh—and then when gently confronted with some probing questions—they realized they were rather fuzzy on their strategy. *A new website won't fix the problem.*

But that's common. And that's when the fun—and the spiritual discernment—kicks in!

We resonate with A.G. Lafley and Roger L. Martin, authors of *Playing to Win: How Strategy Really Works*, who note this myth about chasing after best practices:

"Every industry has tools and practices that become widespread and generic. Some organizations define strategy as benchmarking against competition and then doing the same set of activities but more effectively.

**"Sameness isn't strategy.
It is a recipe for mediocrity."[14]**

---

[14] A.G. Lafley and Roger L. Martin, *Playing to Win: How Strategy Really Works* (Boston: Harvard Business School Publishing, 2013), 5.

3. THE STRATEGY BUCKET

CORE COMPETENCY

> **"We plan, believing the results are up to God.** We energize our people and customers with a Big Holy Audacious Goal (BHAG). We're systematic—never negligent—in our strategic planning. We know our mission statement by memory, and our programs, products and services are in alignment with the mission."

Strategic Balls in the Strategy Bucket

❶ BUILD a team-crafted strategic vision statement.

❷ MEMORIZE your mission statement.

❸ BE STRATEGIC about strategic planning.

❹ SUMMARIZE your plan with a G.N.O.M.E. chart.

SELF-ASSESSMENT:

☑ **Where is your ORGANIZATION or DEPT. today? What's your 1-year goal?**

	4 LEVELS OF MANAGEMENT KNOWLEDGE AND COMPETENCIES	TODAY	IN 1 YEAR:
Level 1	I don't know what I don't know.		
Level 2	I know what I don't know.		
Level 3	I have an action plan to address what I know I don't know.		
Level 4	I am knowledgeable and effective in this core competency and can mentor others.		

☑ **Where are YOU today? What's your 1-year goal?**

	4 LEVELS OF MANAGEMENT KNOWLEDGE AND COMPETENCIES	TODAY	IN 1 YEAR:
Level 1	I don't know what I don't know.		
Level 2	I know what I don't know.		
Level 3	I have an action plan to address what I know I don't know.		
Level 4	I am knowledgeable and effective in this core competency and can mentor others.		

Build a Team-Crafted BHAG!

Ignite the Awesome Power of a Big Holy Audacious Goal!

Jim Collins popularized the BHAG (Big Hairy Audacious Goal) in his book, *Built to Last.* But John Naisbitt hammered the concept home in his 1982 book, *Megatrends.* He wrote "Strategic planning is worthless—unless there is first a strategic vision."

According to NASA, "History changed on October 4, 1957, when the Soviet Union successfully launched Sputnik I. The world's first artificial satellite was about the size of a basketball, weighed only 183 pounds, and took about 98 minutes to orbit the Earth on its elliptical path."

On May 25, 1961, President John F. Kennedy announced what Naisbitt calls a strategic vision:

"Put a man on the moon by 1970!"

"This strategic vision gave **magnetic direction** to the entire organization. Nobody had to be told or reminded of where the organization was going," wrote Naisbitt.[15]

Contrast that strategic vision with this wimpy mission statement:

"We are going to be the world leader in space exploration."
(This doesn't organize anything!)

Discuss: Share one or two examples of strategic vision statements or BHAGs (faith-based organizations may prefer, "Big HOLY Audacious Goal."

RESOURCES:

❑ **The Strategy Bucket: www.managementbuckets.com/strategy-bucket**
❑ *Built to Last: Successful Habits of Visionary Companies*, by Jim Collins and Jerry I. Porras
❑ *The ONE Thing: The Surprisingly Simple Truth Behind Extraordinary Results,* by Gary Keller with Jay Papasan

TO DO OR TO DELEGATE:

Point Person	Task	Deadline	Done!

Bucket Bottom Line:
Every single person on your team (staff, volunteers, donors, envelope-stuffers, past board chairs—plus all of their spouses and/or families) will be energized by your focused BHAG. Or...they will have that deer-in-the-headlights look if your strategic vision is the least bit fuzzy.

---

[15] John Naisbitt, *Megatrends: Ten New Directions Transforming Our Lives* (NY: Warner Books, 1985)

Memorize Your Mission Statement

If your team members cannot recite your mission statement from memory, take it off the wall and rewrite it.

Without looking for the answers, write the following:

Our mission is to…

Our slogan (or brand promise) is…

Our core values are…

RESOURCES:

❑ *101 Mission Statements from Top Companies: Plus Guidelines for Writing Your Own Mission Statement*, by Jeffrey Abrahams
❑ *Peter Drucker's The Five Most Important Questions Self-Assessment Tool: Participant Workbook*, published by Frances Hesselbein Leadership Institute/Jossey-Bass

TO DO OR TO DELEGATE:

Point Person	Task	Deadline	Done!

Bucket Bottom Line:
Your mission statement should fit on a t-shirt. Your slogan (brand promise) should appear everywhere (newsletters, stationery, reception center, etc.), but your VALUES should be lived out day after day after day after day.

Is it time to re-visit the mission statement?

Top-10 Ingredients That Create an Eloquent and Arresting Mission Statement Our mission...	YES! ABSOLUTELY!	TO SOME EXTENT	NOT AT ALL
#1. Is short and easily focused.			
#2. Is clear and easily understood.			
#3. Defines why we do what we do, why the organization exists.			
#4. Does not prescribe means.			
#5. Is sufficiently broad.			
#6. Provides direction for doing the right things.			
#7. Addresses our opportunities.			
#8. Matches our competence.			
#9. Inspires our commitment.			
#10. Says what, in the end, we want to be remembered for.			

Note: These 10 questions are adapted from *The Five Most Important Questions Self-Assessment Tool: Participant Workbook.*[16]

Bonus Question: Does our mission statement...**fit on a T-shirt?**			

Should our mission statement be re-visited?
- ❑ Yes
- ❑ No
- ❑ Maybe

---

[16] Peter F. Drucker, *The Five Most Important Questions Self-Assessment Tool: Participant Workbook, Third Edition* (San Francisco: Jossey-Bass, 2010).

Does our mission statement fit on a T-shirt?

Be Strategic About Strategic Planning

"Insanity is doing the same thing over and over again and expecting different results."

6 Steps from *Mastering the Management Buckets*	**6** Steps from 1 Chronicles 28-29 in *Breakthrough*, by Randon Samuelson*
1) Retain a consultant (or a volunteer).	1) Inspiring Vision
2) Create a rolling three-year plan.	2) A Credible Plan
3) Begin with the basics.	3) The Right Leader
4) Assign a point person.	4) Initial Funding
5) Work through the five "Drucker Questions."	5) Going Public
6) Pray for a breakthrough and read B*reakthrough*	6) Sharing Credit

Must-read!

"One of the best faith-based books on strategy and strategic planning."

John Pearson

*Key Log Question:
"Other than money, what one opportunity (or obstacle) if captured (or removed) would most advance your mission/vision?"

*Author Randy Samelson helps organizations identify key opportunities or obstacles. They focus on the "Key Log."

Borrowing the perfect metaphor from Fred Smith, Sr., he explains: "…in the lumber industry when trees are cut and floated down rivers, they are susceptible to log jams. Over time, the industry learned that through satellite images and computer modeling, they could identify the one key log that if blown-up would release the log jam allowing the logs to move toward their destination."

"Individuals and organizations also experience the equivalent of 'log jams.' Progress is stopped." And Samelson says there are "biblical principles that can be used to identify the key impediment and wise strategies to eliminate it."[17]

RESOURCE:

❑ *Breakthrough: Unleashing the Power of a Proven Plan, by Randon A. Samelson*

TO DO OR TO DELEGATE:

Point Person	Task	Deadline	Done!

Bucket Bottom Line:
"There is in the act of preparing, the moment you start caring." (Winston Churchill)

---

[17] Randon A. Samelson, Breakthrough: Unleashing the Power of a Proven Plan (Colorado Springs, CO: Counsel & Capital, 2014), 19.

Summarize Your Plan With a G.N.O.M.E. Chart

This would have helped Christopher Columbus who did not know where he was going when he left, and did not know where he had been when he returned home!

Read Chapter 3 in *Mastering the Management Buckets* and then begin the strategic planning process by discussing nominees for your 3 to 5 annual goals or, if you prefer, visionary priorities.

GOALS	NEEDS	OBJECTIVES	METHODS*	EVALUATION*
1.				
2.				
3.				
4.				
5.				

*Typically, the board of directors should focus on Goals, Needs, and Objectives (Strategy)—and when crystal clear (and in writing), the board should give freedom for the staff to focus on Methods (Tactics) and Evaluation (reporting back to the board that goals have been achieved in alignment with the vision, mission and core values.

RESOURCES:
❑ *Playing to Win: How Strategy Really Works*, by A.G. Lafley and Roger L. Martin
❑ *Harvard Business Review's 10 Must Reads on Strategy (including the featured article "What Is Strategy?")* by Michael E. Porter

TO DO OR TO DELEGATE:

Point Person	Task	Deadline	Done!

Bucket Bottom Line:
The reason your team doesn't have time to create a strategic plan is because you don't have a strategic plan!

 (continued)

Wordsmith Your Strategic Plan Placemat
Post your 11" x 17" placemat on every wall and in every cubicle!

THE 5 KEY ELEMENTS OF YOUR STRATEGIC PLAN PLACEMAT

1) The **P**rocess
2) The **P**eople
3) The **P**lacemat
4) The **P**roclamation
5) The **P**rogress (accountability and annual update)

THE ROLLING 3-YEAR STRATEGIC PLAN

☑ Mission

☑ Strategic Vision (BHAG)

☑ Core Values

Rolling 3-year plan, updated annually adding 1 more year (see sample on next page):
    ☑ Goal #1
    ☑ Goal #2
    ☑ Goal #3
    ☑ Goal #4
    ☑ Goal #5

**"If you have more than 5 goals,
you have none."**
Peter Drucker

RESOURCES:

❏ Roger L. Martin, "The Big Lie of Strategic Planning: A detailed plan may be comforting, but it's not a strategy." *Harvard Business Review* (Jan/Feb 2014)
❏ A HUGE THANKS to David Schmidt of J. David Schmidt & Associates, Wheaton, IL, for introducing us to the strategic plan placemat concept. Visit: www.WisePlanning.net

TO DO OR TO DELEGATE:

Point Person	Task	Deadline	Done!

Bucket Bottom Line:
The Strategic Plan Placemat will revolutionize the routine of your paid and unpaid team members when you inspire them to connect the BHAG with their day-to-day faithfulness.

STRATEGIC PLAN PLACEMAT – TEMPLATE
[Recommended: 11" x 17" landscape - color placemat for every team member]

"Commit your actions to the Lord, and your plans will success." (Proverbs 16:3 NLT)

XYZ International's Strategic Plan: 2018 – 2020

(logo)	(slogan)
MISSION Why we exist.	Our mission is to…
VALUES How we will treat each other and our constituents.	We value: • _____ • _____ • _____
VISION What we want to be in the future.	
BHAG Not achievable without God's unique blessing	By _____, 2025, our Big HOLY Audacious Goal is to… Note: The BHAG should be written as a "SMART Goal" and be measurable, memorable, and succinct. (For balance, read *The Choice: The Christ-Centered Pursuit of Kingdom Outcomes*.)

Visionary Priorities The Rolling 3-Year Plan is updated annually by Nov. 15➔	Year 1: **2018**	Year 2: **2019**	Year 3: **2020**	Add **2021** by 11/15/2018
#1: (verb)… **TO BUILD** a…	• _____ • _____ • _____	• _____ • _____ • _____	• _____ • _____ • _____	
#2: (verb)… **TO CREATE** a…	• _____ • _____ • _____	• _____ • _____ • _____	• _____ • _____ • _____	
#3: (verb)… **TO ENRICH** a…	• _____ • _____ • _____	• _____ • _____ • _____	• _____ • _____ • _____	

S.M.A.R.T. Goals are: **S**pecific, **M**easurable, **A**chievable, **R**ealistic, and **T**ime-related

Strategic Plan Placemat: Version 1.0 (Nov. 15, 2017). This Rolling 3-Year Strategic Plan is updated annually by November 15 and is ready for board approval at the year-end board meeting.

See sample 11" x 17" (landscape format) strategic plan placemat example on next page➔

Strategic plan placemat example: 11" x 17" (landscape format)

AMBASSADORS FOOTBALL

FOOTBALL ◆ FAITH ◆ FUTURE

The Rolling 3-Year Strategic Plan ▪ 2016 to 2018

MISSION	OUR MISSION IS TO COMMUNICATE THE GOOD NEWS OF JESUS TO ALL PEOPLE THROUGH FOOTBALL.
VISION	OUR VISION IS THE TRANSFORMATION OF INDIVIDUALS AND COMMUNITIES THROUGH INDIGENOUS FOOTBALL OUTREACH.
VALUES	1) We value FOOTBALL: We participate in football at all levels with passion, excellence and respect. 2) We value CHURCH: We uphold the long-term, transformative role of the Church in the world. 3) We value TEAM: We identify and collaborate with others in the pursuit of shared goals. 4) We value SERVICE: We follow the example of Jesus by leading through service and prioritising the marginalised.
BHAG	Our Big Holy Audacious Goal: By December 31, 20___, to...

VISIONARY PRIORITIES→	2016 BUILD (START WITH A VERB...)	2017 CREATE (START WITH A VERB...)	2018 SUSTAIN (START WITH A VERB...)
GOAL #1	#1. Enrich ___ so that there are ___ more than ___ (units) serving us base)	#1. Enrich ___ By Dec. 31, 2017, enrich ___ so that there are ___ more than ___ (units) serving us base)	#1. Enrich ___ By Dec. 31, 2018, enrich ___ so that there are ___ more than ___ (units) serving us base)
GOAL #2	#2. Grow ___ By Dec. 31, 2016, grow ___ so that there are ___ more than ___ (units) serving us base) Example: Example: Example:	#2. Grow ___ By Dec. 31, 2017, grow ___ so that there are ___ more than ___ (units) serving us base) Example: Example: Example:	#2. Grow ___ By Dec. 31, 2018, grow ___ so that there are ___ more than ___ (units) serving us base) Example: Example: Example:
GOAL #3	#3. Research ___ By June 30, 2016, research ___ to create ___ (new should launch XYZ Programs in 2017. Example: Example: Example:	#3. Research ___ By Dec. 31, 2017, research it the first step, continue or grow in 2018/19. Example: Example: Example:	#3. Research ___ By April 30, 2018, realise ___ Example: Example: Example:

| | | | | 2019 to be added by Nov. 15, 2016 |

S.M.A.R.T. GOALS ARE: Specific, Measurable, Achievable, Realistic, Time-related

EXAMPLE ONLY: The template on the previous page is just that—a template. Use the categories, if helpful, or create your own categories. If possible, begin each goal with a VERB (enrich, grow, research, engage, retain, abandon, pray, train, build, etc.). The final approved version will be the one-page summary of other documents, often including 3-5 "SMART Goals" for every team member, and monthly "dashboard" reporting templates.

Ambassadors Football (Example Only: Used by permission.)

	Year 1: 2016
VISIONARY PRIORITIES➜	BUILD A GLOBAL EVANGELISM MOVEMENT BY INSPIRING AND EQUIPPING 35 COUNTRIES WITH AMBASSADORS FOOTBALL EXPERTISE AND RESOURCES BY DEC. 31, 2018.
GOAL #1	**#1. Enrich Current Country Relationships:** By Dec. 31, 2016, enrich the international work and scope of AF so that all 25 country leaders (and their indigenous boards) rate AF support and services at 4.0 on a scale of 1 to 5 (5.0 is excellent).
GOAL #2	**#2. Grow by 3 Countries:** By Dec. 31, 2016, welcome at least 3 new country relationships (for a total of 28 total countries)—and affirm that the new countries have met the criteria per the "XYZ Relationship" document, to include: ▪ Indigenous board of at least ___ people. ▪ Three-year sustainability plan ▪ Partner Relationship with a current AF Country
GOAL #3	**#3. Research & Teach Best Practices:** By June 30, 2016, research the best practices of AF's strongest countries and document 3 to 5 country models for effective ministry and create a 2017-2018 strategy for training these models/best practices to the other current and new countries. ▪ Example: Case Study or Online Course or Webinars ▪ Example: Consultant Team (of current country directors) ▪ Example: Regional "McDonald's University" model ▪ And…identify 2-4 other international ministry organizations that have moved from 25 to 50 countries (and how they did it).

Read more about Ambassadors Football, a unique international organization ministering through football (soccer) around the world.
www.ambassadorsfootball.org

News Flash! First Covenant Church Unveils New Mission Statement

VISALIA, Calif. — First Covenant Church unveiled a new mission statement last week, hoping to launch the church into an era of greater unity and spiritual effectiveness.

But response to the two-page statement has been decidedly mixed among church members who despair of memorizing it as the church has requested.

"It's a verbal tangle of quasi-eloquent nothingness," grumbles one man. "I can't even say it right when it's projected on the screen. I end up with a mouthful of blah."

The new statement reads:

> **First Covenant Church** exists for the passion and purpose of inspiring, discipling, equipping and sending out Christ followers with the destiny of transforming the world to the glory of God the Father, Son and Holy Spirit, and fostering a graceful yet convicting church environment in which people of all faith experiences and backgrounds are molded into the image and reflection of Christ, together creating a God-honoring community of authentic worshipers deliberately focused on reaching their community, the nation, the next generation of believers and the world through missions works, innovative programs and prayer.

And that's just the first sentence.

The church has gone into a full-court press to get members to memorize the statement. The full text is posted on every door in the church, in bathroom stalls, in the bulletin and on all church correspondence and emails. The church is running a half-page ad featuring the statement in the local newspaper for two weeks. They were unable to fit it into their usual quarter-page space.

Services now begin with everyone holding up their Bibles and reading the statement off the screens together with the pastor. All church-sanctioned events, from small groups to softball games, must now begin with participants reciting it together.

"It takes longer to get through than the national anthem," says one softball team captain. "The other teams laugh at us."

Pastor Jack Lewine says he felt obligated to promote the statement mainly because his associate pastor Glen Pamplin had labored over it for six months before presenting it to the church. But even Lewine admits he had to delay the unveiling for two weeks so he could "get my own head around it." He can now recite it in less than 90 seconds, of which he is proud.

Pamplin is reportedly irritated by people's "reluctance to get on board with what God is doing at First Covenant." He says the statement's length simply reflects that God has a lot in store for the church in the future. Bristling at the criticism, Pamplin recently floated the idea of throwing a contest with a cash prize to see if anyone in the congregation can come up with a better statement "that still fully encompasses, embodies and encourages our fundamental mission as an outpost of grace, joy and love for Christ in the city to which he has called us at this time in history," he says.

Suggestions are already rolling in.

"How about, 'Jesus rules,'" says one seventh grader. "They should pay me by how many words I didn't use."[18]

#4: THE DRUCKER BUCKET

Many of our clients are millennials who enjoy bringing new insights, new approaches, and new strategies to their causes.

So sometimes we get pushback when we suggest their lifelong learning disciplines ought to include reading and listening to the wisdom of Peter Drucker, "the father of modern management." ("Father" sounds old in any language!)

But when I remind millennials that there is much wisdom from the "Old" Testament and from the writers of Scripture (who died two millennia ago), they soften.

Many leaders get a "daily dose of Drucker" by reading *The Daily Drucker: 366 Days of Insight and Motivation for Getting the Right Things Done*[19]. We also love to inspire our clients with our favorite Druckerisms:[20]

❑ **"People who don't take risks generally make about two big mistakes a year. People who do take risks generally make about two big mistakes a year."**

❑ "No institution can possibly survive if it needs geniuses or supermen to manage it. It must be organized in such a way as to be able to get along under a leadership composed of average human beings."

❑ "We now accept the fact that learning is a lifelong process of keeping abreast of change. And the most pressing task is to teach people how to learn."

❑ "Plans are only good intentions unless they immediately degenerate into hard work."

---

[19] Peter F. Drucker with Joseph A. Maciariello, *The Daily Drucker: 366 Days of Insight and Motivation for Getting the Right Things Done* (New York: HarperCollins, 2004).

[20] http://www.brainyquote.com/quotes/authors/p/peter_f_drucker.html

4. THE DRUCKER BUCKET

CORE COMPETENCY

We are privileged to be leaders and managers and we steward that privilege by being lifelong learners and practitioners in the art of management. We don't just give lip service to management—we are disciplined students of great leadership and management thinkers like Peter Drucker, Ken Blanchard and others.

Strategic Balls in the Drucker Bucket

❶ LEAD from your strengths.

❷ PRACTICE the art of management.

❸ READ or re-read one Drucker book each year.

SELF-ASSESSMENT:

☑ **Where is your ORGANIZATION or DEPT. today? What's your 1-year goal?**

	4 LEVELS OF MANAGEMENT KNOWLEDGE AND COMPETENCIES	TODAY	IN 1 YEAR:
Level 1	I don't know what I don't know.		
Level 2	I know what I don't know.		
Level 3	I have an action plan to address what I know I don't know.		
Level 4	I am knowledgeable and effective in this core competency and can mentor others.		

☑ **Where are YOU today? What's your 1-year goal?**

	4 LEVELS OF MANAGEMENT KNOWLEDGE AND COMPETENCIES	TODAY	IN 1 YEAR:
Level 1	I don't know what I don't know.		
Level 2	I know what I don't know.		
Level 3	I have an action plan to address what I know I don't know.		
Level 4	I am knowledgeable and effective in this core competency and can mentor others.		

① Lead From Your Strengths

Peter Drucker launched a movement to minimize weaknesses.

Peter F. Drucker, the father of modern management, was welcomed into his heavenly home on Nov. 11, 2005, just a few days shy of his 96th birthday. According to Bob Buford (www.bobbuford.com), "his last days were consumed with repeating the Lord's Prayer in German."

Christian Management Association honored Peter Drucker with its highest honor, the Christian Management Award, in 1990. CMA honored Bob Buford with the same award in 2005. I must mention Drucker and Buford in the same breath because it was Buford, and his Leadership Network (www.leadnet.org), that brought much of Drucker's wisdom and management insight to the leading Christian leaders and senior pastors of our day.

Certainly one of my Top 10 Life Experiences was sitting at the feet of Peter Drucker for a week in Estes Park, Colo., with 30 other Christian leaders in the summer of 1986. Buford invited us. Drucker enthralled us. Several years later, I was privileged to be part of a reunion week with Drucker in Claremont, Calif. My notes from those weeks would fill several books—but one Big Idea stands out:

Lead From Your Strengths!

It sounds simple, but it's radical. Focus on your strengths, not your weaknesses. Figure out who you are, what you enjoy doing, what you're good at—and then build a team around you to fill in the cracks. Don't allow anyone else's leadership theory to take your eye off the ball. Lead from your strengths.

I've dedicated one of my 20 Management Buckets to Peter Drucker. "The Drucker Bucket" really transcends all the buckets—but we must talk about the Druckerisms and the wit and wisdom of this remarkable management guru. He was a gift from God to ministry leaders. He was a category of one.

Discuss: What are your Top-5 Strengths (see the Team Bucket)? Do your colleagues and your boss help you leverage your strengths every day?

RESOURCES:

❑ **The Drucker Bucket: http://managementbuckets.com/drucker-bucket**
❑ Drucker Institute - www.drucker.institute
❑ *The Effective Executive: The Definitive Guide to Getting the Right Things Done*, by Peter F. Drucker
❑ *The Daily Drucker: 366 Days of Insight and Motivation for Getting the Right Things Done, by* Peter F. Drucker
❑ *Drucker & Me: What a Texas Entrepreneur Learned from the Father of Modern Management,* by Bob Buford

TO DO OR TO DELEGATE:

Point Person	Task	Deadline	Done!

Practice the Art of Management

Exercise your management muscles with a daily dose of Drucker.

Read *The Daily Drucker* daily!
5 Ways to Leverage This Book and Practice, Practice, Practice the Art of Management

5 Ways:	Assignment: Pick one you will do and pick one you will delegate:
#1. Stand and read.	
#2. Boot and read.	
#3. Email and read.	
#4. Post and read.	
#5. Brown bag and read.	

RESOURCES:

❑ *The Daily Drucker: 366 Days of Insight and Motivation for Getting the Right Things Done,* by Peter F. Drucker
❑ *A Year with Peter Drucker: 52 Weeks of Coaching for Leadership Effectiveness,* by Joseph A. Maciariello
❑ Weekly Blog (2015): "Drucker Mondays" Visit:
    www.urgentink.typepad.com/drucker_mondays
❑ *Managing the Nonprofit Organization: Principles and Practices,* by Peter F. Drucker
❑ *Leadership Is an Art, by* Max De Pree

TO DO OR TO DELEGATE:

Point Person	Task	Deadline	Done!

Bucket Bottom Line:
To practice and execute the art of management, you must commit time and thought. Create your own disciplined process for mastering the 20 management bucket competencies. Your plan might involve 20 days, 20 weeks, 20 months or 20 years. Make a plan. Just do it!

Read (or Re-read)…
One Peter Drucker Book Each Year
The father of modern management knows best.

Drucker wrote 2 novels!

Books by Peter F. Drucker, the Father of Modern Management[21]

DRUCKER'S 39 BOOKS:

- The End of Economic Man (1939)
- The Future of Industrial Man (1942)
- Concept of the Corporation (1946)
- The New Society (1950)
- The Practice of Management (1954)
- America's Next Twenty Years (1957)
- Landmarks of Tomorrow (1957)
- Managing for Results (1964)
- The Effective Executive (1966)
- The Age of Discontinuity (1968)
- Technology, Management and Society (1970)
- The New Markets and Other Essays (1971)
- Men, Ideas and Politics (1971)
- Drucker on Management (1971)
- Management: Tasks, Responsibilities, Practices (1973)
- The Unseen Revolution (1976; reissued in 1996 under the title The Pension Fund Revolution)
- People and Performance: The Best of Peter Drucker on Management (1977)
- Adventures of a Bystander (1978)
- Managing in Turbulent Times (1980)
- Toward the Next Economics and Other Essays (1981)
- The Changing World of the Executive (1982)
- The Last of All Possible Worlds (1982)
- The Temptation to Do Good (1984)
- Innovation and Entrepreneurship (1985)
- Frontiers of Management (1986)
- The New Realities: in Government and Politics, in Economics and Business, in Society and World View (1989)
- Managing the Nonprofit Organization: Principles and Practices (1990)
- Managing for the Future (1992)
- The Ecological Vision (1993)
- Post-Capitalist Society (1993)
- Managing in a Time of Great Change (1995)
- Drucker on Asia: A Dialogue between Peter Drucker and Isao Nakauchi (1997)
- Peter Drucker on the Profession of Management (1998)
- Management Challenges for the 21st Century (1999)
- The Essential Drucker (2001)
- Managing in the Next Society (2002)
- A Functioning Society (2002)
- The Daily Drucker (2004, with Joseph A. Maciariello)
- The Five Most Important Questions (2008; posthumously released)

RESOURCES:

- *A Class With Drucker: The Lost Lessons of the World's Greatest Management Teacher,* by William A. Cohen
- *The Practical Drucker: Applying the Wisdom of the World's Greatest Management Thinker,* by William A. Cohen

TO DO OR TO DELEGATE:

Point Person	Task	Deadline	Done!

Bucket Bottom Line:
We all need outside help and coaching. Peter Drucker said, "My greatest strength as a consultant is to be ignorant and ask a few questions."

---

[21] http://www.druckerinstitute.com/peter-druckers-life-and-legacy/books-by-drucker/

 Bonus Ball!

Quote Drucker—and Inspire Your Team!
Use the right Druckerism at the right time for the right reason.

Peter F. Drucker Quotes[22]

As Bob Buford reminded us in the foreword
to *Mastering the Management Buckets*, Drucker said,
**"The purpose of management is not to make the Church more businesslike,
but more Church-like."**

❑ Management by objective works—if you know the objectives. Ninety percent of the time you don't.

❑ Accept the fact that we have to treat almost anybody as a volunteer.

❑ Company cultures are like country cultures. Never try to change one. Try, instead, to work with what you've got.

❑ Effective leadership is not about making speeches or being liked; leadership is defined by results not attributes.

❑ Efficiency is doing things right; effectiveness is doing the right things.

❑ Executives owe it to the organization and to their fellow workers not to tolerate nonperforming individuals in important jobs.

❑ Follow effective action with quiet reflection. From the quiet reflection will come even more effective action.

❑ Most of what we call management consists of making it difficult for people to get their work done.

❑ No institution can possibly survive if it needs geniuses or supermen to manage it. It must be organized in such a way as to be able to get along under a leadership composed of average human beings.

❑ People who don't take risks generally make about two big mistakes a year. People who do take risks generally make about two big mistakes a year.

**"What everyone knows
is usually wrong."**

---

[22] http://www.brainyquote.com/quotes/authors/p/peter_f_drucker.html

❑ Plans are only good intentions unless they immediately degenerate into hard work.

❑ At least once every five years, every form should be put on trial for its life.

❑ Rank does not confer privilege or give power. It imposes responsibility.

❑ The aim of marketing is to know and understand the customer so well the product or service fits him and sells itself.

❑ The best way to predict the future is to create it.

❑ The most important thing in communication is hearing what isn't said.

❑ The productivity of work is not the responsibility of the worker but of the manager.

❑ The purpose of business is to create and keep a customer.

❑ There is an enormous number of managers who have retired on the job.

❑ There is nothing so useless as doing efficiently that which should not be done at all.

❑ Time is the scarcest resource and unless it is managed nothing else can be managed.

❑ We now accept the fact that learning is a lifelong process of keeping abreast of change. And the most pressing task is to teach people how to learn.

❑ When a subject becomes totally obsolete we make it a required course.

TO DO OR TO DELEGATE:

Point Person	Task	Deadline	Done!

Bucket Bottom Line:
When consulting with Jack Welch (who grew GE from $12 billion to more than 25 times that figure), Drucker challenged Welch with two questions:
  • "If GE wasn't already in a particular business, would you enter it today?"
  • "If the answer is no, what are you going to do about it?"
Read more in Chapter 30, "Drucker's Theory of Abandonment" in *The Practical Drucker.*[23]

---

[23] William A. Cohen, *The Practical Drucker: Applying the Wisdom of the World's Greatest Management Thinker* (New York: AMACOM, a division of American Management Association, 2014), 188.

Graphic from page 72 of *Mastering the Management Buckets*[24]

---

[24] http://www.brainyquote.com/quotes/authors/p/peter_f_drucker.html

#5: THE BOOK BUCKET

Gary Keller:

> "A college professor once told me, 'Gary, you're smart, but people have lived before you. You're not the first person to dream big, so you'd be wise to study what others have learned first, and then build your actions on the back of their lessons.'"[25]

"ROLE MODELS FOR SUCCESS"

Gary Keller, author of John Pearson's 2016 "Book-of-the-Year" pick, a *New York Times* bestseller, is a big fan of books:

"One of the reasons I've amassed a large library of books over the years is because books are a great go-to resource. Short of having a conversation with someone who has accomplished what you hope to achieve, in my experience books and published works offer the most in terms of documented research and role models for success."[26]

Why are books so powerful? Maybe this humorous note from Anatole France will give you a clue:

"Never lend books, for no one ever returns them; the only books I have in my library are books that other folk have lent me."[27]

---

[25] Gary Keller with Jay Papasan, *The ONE Thing: The Surprisingly Simple Truth Behind Extraordinary Results* (Austin, TX: Bard, 2012), 125.
[26] Ibid., 125.
[27] Charlie "Tremendous" Jones, *Books Are Tremendous* (Mechanicsburg, PA: Executive Books, 2004), 14.

5. THE BOOK BUCKET
CORE COMPETENCY

> **We believe leaders are readers!** We create a culture that embraces a healthy appetite for leadership and management books, journals, articles and audio resources. We mentor team members with thoughtfully selected titles and chapters to help them leverage their strengths, grow in their faith and serve others with passion. We don't just talk about books—we actually read them!

Strategic Balls in the Book Bucket

❶ AVOID management-by-bestseller syndrome.

❷ MENTOR your team members with niche books.

❸ MASTER the management buckets by reading.

❹ CREATE your top-100 books list.

SELF-ASSESSMENT:

☑ **Where is your ORGANIZATION or DEPT. today? What's your 1-year goal?**

	4 LEVELS OF MANAGEMENT KNOWLEDGE AND COMPETENCIES	TODAY	IN 1 YEAR:
Level 1	I don't know what I don't know.		
Level 2	I know what I don't know.		
Level 3	I have an action plan to address what I know I don't know.		
Level 4	I am knowledgeable and effective in this core competency and can mentor others.		

☑ **Where are YOU today? What's your 1-year goal?**

	4 LEVELS OF MANAGEMENT KNOWLEDGE AND COMPETENCIES	TODAY	IN 1 YEAR:
Level 1	I don't know what I don't know.		
Level 2	I know what I don't know.		
Level 3	I have an action plan to address what I know I don't know.		
Level 4	I am knowledgeable and effective in this core competency and can mentor others.		

① Avoid Management-by-Bestseller Syndrome

Management gimmick-of-the-month whiplash can be fatal!

Quick! Pick the management "hot button" topic that is the best:

❑ Blue Ocean Strategy
❑ Myers-Briggs, DISC, StrengthsFinder, Social Styles, LOGB, Birkman, Enneagram
❑ Emotional Intelligence
❑ Balanced Scorecard
❑ Benchmarking
❑ Management by Objectives (MBO)
❑ Management by Wandering Around *(wondering around?)*
❑ Values-based Management
❑ Diversity-focused Leadership

❑ Six Sigma
❑ TQM
❑ SWOT
❑ BHAGs, Stretch Goals, SMART Goals
❑ **Or maybe:** Drucker, Blanchard, Collins, Lencioni, Engstrom, Bakke, Deming, Laurie Beth Jones, Hybels, Warren or Maxwell?

HELP!

I first heard the phrase "management-by-bestseller" over coffee at Starbucks with Scott Vandeventer, then chief operating officer at Evangelical Christian Credit Union. He commented, "Too many leaders frolic from fad to fad, taking otherwise good ideas and making programs out of them for as long as their attention spans can handle it, without ever getting to their core values and their own unique business model or value proposition." Scott nailed it.

He added, "The issue isn't that the concepts are lightweight—they're often quite good—but when the leader is ever-searching, they never get to the root issues behind their search. We wouldn't describe *Good to Great* by Jim Collins as 'lite.' It has great ideas, but leaders jump into the ideas as if every single one applies to their case. That's a major error. They need to ask what they can take from the book into their world.

Some organizations get dangerously close to
Management-by-Bestseller Syndrome
due to a kind of corporate attention deficit disorder,
probably systemic to its leadership."

Assignment: Start your "Leadership/Management Books Wish List" at Amazon.com.

RESOURCES:

❑ **The Book Bucket: www.managementbuckets.com/book-bucket**
❑ John Pearson's Buckets Blog (350+ book reviews): www.urgentink.typepad.com

TO DO OR TO DELEGATE:

Point Person	Task	Deadline	Done!

Mentor Your Team Members With Niche Books

Leverage their strengths with thoughtfully selected chapters.

Management Challenge	Niche Book or Chapter
➜ Rookie manager needs to learn the importance of affirming team members.	*The New One Minute Manager*, by Ken Blanchard and Spencer Johnson, M.D.
➜ Faulty sequential view of priorities (God first, family second, church third, career fourth)	*Balancing Life's Demands: A New Perspective on Priorities*, by J. Grant Howard
➜ Building trust with team members	*The Carrot Principle: How the Best Managers Use Recognition to Engage Their People, Retain Talent, and Accelerate Performance*, by Adrian Gostick and Chester Elton (Note: Chapter 10 has 125 recognition ideas.)
➜ Team member with workaholic tendencies and imbalanced life	*When Work and Family Collide: Keeping Your Job from Cheating Your Family*, by Andy Stanley
➜ I don't understand my boss, my board members or my direct reports. (What makes them tick?)	*Strengths Finder 2.0*, by Tom Rath
Your Suggestions:	

RESOURCES:

❑ *The Ideal Team Player: How to Recognize and Cultivate the Three Essential Virtues*, by Patrick M. Lencioni (John Pearson's runner-up to his 2016 book-of-the-year)
❑ *FYI: For Your Improvement, A Guide for Development and Coaching* (4th Edition), by Michael M. Lombardo and Robert W. Eichinger

TO DO OR TO DELEGATE:

Point Person	Task	Deadline	Done!

③ Master the Management Buckets by Reading

Put down the duckie!

Order from Amazon:
http://amzn.to/2wwd4Dm

View on YouTube:
https://www.youtube.com/
watch?v=2-me6PYnDJ0

If you grew up in the first Sesame Street era or are blessed with children or grandchildren, you may remember the hilarious upbeat tune, "Put Down the Duckie," that featured more than a dozen celebrities and musicians, including Paul Simon, John Candy and Danny DeVito. Jazzman Hoots the Owl is teaching Ernie to play the saxophone, but Ernie won't put down his rubber yellow duckie. Hoots sings,

**"You gotta put down the duckie.
Put down the duckie.
Put down the duckie,
if you wanna play the saxophone!"**

That's the message in the Book Bucket. If you're passionate about your mission and your BHAG, you must practice, practice and practice the art of management. In essence, you must **"lay aside every weight and the sin which so easily ensnares us"** (Heb. 12:1, NIV) if you want to lead and manage with excellence.

What duckie are you willing to put down today so you can pick up a book and be a leader of excellence? Mastering the 20 management buckets may seem overwhelming to your team members—maybe even to you. But how do you eat an elephant? One bite at a time.

Start with three buckets and three books. Don't procrastinate. Start today. Identify the three buckets you'd like to master first and get one book recommendation for each bucket (from my list at the end of this workbook, or from a peer or mentor). Read those three titles in the next 90 days.

Bucket #1: _____
Book: _____

Bucket #2: _____
Book: _____

Bucket #3: _____
Book: _____

TO DO OR TO DELEGATE:

Point Person	Task	Deadline	Done!

20 Books to Get You Started!

John Pearson's pick for 2016 Book-of-the-Year

***The ONE Thing: The Surprisingly Simple Truth Behind Extraordinary Results*, by Gary Keller with Jay Papasan**

**"What's the ONE Thing
you can do this week such that by doing it
everything else would be easier or unnecessary?"**

Read John's review:
http://urgentink.typepad.com/my_weblog/2016/05/the-one-thing.html

John Pearson's "Top-20 Books" and "Top-100 Books" (updated annually) are not prescriptive for every leader or manager. The list represents an assortment of well-known and lesser-known leadership and management books that John often recommends to clients. The list changes every year—but many books remain on the list every year. For John's original list of his Top-100 books, read the "Book Bucket" chapter in *Mastering the Management Buckets*.

OUR CAUSE

❑ **1. The Results Bucket:** *The Three Signs of a Miserable Job: A Fable for Managers (and Their Employees)*, by Patrick Lencioni

❑ **2. The Customer Bucket:** *Peter Drucker's Five Most Important Questions: Enduring Wisdom for Today's Leaders*, by Peter F. Drucker, Frances Hesselbein, and Joan Snyder Kuhl

❑ **3. The Strategy Bucket:** *Breakthrough: Unleashing the Power of a Proven Plan*, by Randon A. Samelson

❑ **4. The Drucker Bucket:** *The Daily Drucker: 366 Days of Insight and Motivation for Getting the Right Things Done, by* Peter F. Drucker with Joseph A. Maciariello

❑ **5. The Book Bucket:** *The Best Question Ever: A Revolutionary Approach to Decision Making*, by Andy Stanley

❑ **6. The Program Bucket:** *Marketing Your Ministry: Ten Critical Principles*, by John W. Pearson and Robert D. Hisrich

OUR COMMUNITY

❑ **7. The People Bucket:** *How to Deal With Annoying People: What to Do When You Can't Avoid Them*, by Bob Phillips

❑ **8. The Culture Bucket:** *The Ideal Team Player: How to Recognize and Cultivate the Three Essential Virtues,* by Patrick M. Lencioni (runner-up to John's 2016 book-of-the-year)

❑ **9. The Team Bucket:** *StrengthsFinder 2.0*, by Tom Rath

❑ **10. The *Hoopla!* Bucket:** *Joy at Work: A Revolutionary Approach to Fun on the Job*, by Dennis Bakke

❑ **11. The Donor Bucket:** *Development 101: Building a Comprehensive Development Program on Biblical Values*, by John R. Frank and R. Scott Rodin

❑ **12. The Volunteer Bucket:** *Simply Strategic Volunteers: Empowering People for Ministry*, by Tony Morgan and Tim Stevens

❑ **13. The Crisis Bucket:** *The Effective Executive: The Definitive Guide to Getting the Right Things Done*, by Peter F. Drucker

OUR CORPORATION

❑ **14. The Board Bucket:** *Lessons From the Nonprofit Boardroom*, by Dan Busby and John Pearson (coming Fall 2017, ECFAPress, www.ECFA.org)

❑ **15. The Budget Bucket:** *Zondervan 2018 Church and Nonprofit Tax and Financial Guide: For 2017 Tax Returns*, Dan Busby, Michael Martin, and John Van Drunen

❑ **16. The Delegation Bucket:** *The One Minute Manager Meets the Monkey*, by Ken Blanchard, William Oncken, and Hal Burrows

❑ **17. The Operations Bucket:** *The Minister's MBA: Essential Business Tools for Maximum Ministry Success*, by George S. Babbes and Michael Zigarelli

❑ **18. The Systems Bucket:** *The E-Myth: Why Most Small Businesses Don't Work and What to Do About It*, by Michael E. Gerber

❑ **19. The Printing Bucket:** *Associated Press (AP) Stylebook and Briefing on Media Law*, published by the Associated Press

❑ **20. The Meetings Bucket:** *Death by Meeting: A Leadership Fable...About Solving the Most Painful Problem in Business*, by Patrick M. Lencioni

RESOURCES: Book Reviews from *Your Weekly Staff Meeting* eNews
John Pearson, Editor & Publisher

❑ Download three book lists posted at: www.managementbuckets.com/book-bucket
    Updated Annually:
    ✓ List #1: Books by Management Buckets Category
    ✓ List #2: Books by eNews Issue Number
    ✓ List #3: John Top-100 Book List

❑ Subscribe to *Your Weekly Staff Meeting eNews,* edited and published by John Pearson—with up to three issues per month, each with a book review and a color commentary on one of the management buckets.
    ✓ **Subscribe:** www.managementbuckets.com/enews
    ✓ **eNews archives:** www.urgentink.typepad.com

Create Your Top-100 Books List

Pick your Top-3, Top-10, and Top-100 books.

Your Name_____

Your Goal _____

Top 100 List	☑ When Read	Title, Author, Date	Best Chapter(s) and "Niche Notes"
1			
2			
3			
4			
5			
6			
7			
8			
9			
10			
11			
12			
13			
14			
15			
16			
17			
18			
19			
20			
21			
22			
23			
24			
25			
26			
27			
28			
29			
30			
31			
32			
33			
34			
35			
36			
37			

38			
39			
40			
41			
42			
43			
44			
45			
46			
47			
48			
49			
50			
51			
52			
53			
54			
55			
56			
57			
58			
59			
60			
61			
62			
63			
64			
65			
66			
67			
68			
69			
70			
71			
72			
73			
74			
75			
76			
77			
78			
79			
80			
81			
82			
83			
84			
85			
86			
87			

88			
89			
90			
91			
92			
93			
94			
95			
96			
97			
98			
99			
100			

I will host the following *Hoopla!* Event when I complete my 100th book!

TO DO OR TO DELEGATE:

Point Person	Task	Deadline	Done!

Bucket Bottom Line:
C.S. Lewis: "It is a good rule after reading a new book, never to allow yourself another new one till you have read an old one in between."[28]

---

[28] http://merecslewis.blogspot.com/2011/01/on-reading-of-old-christian-books.html

#6: THE PROGRAM BUCKET

> "When the only two answers are yes or no, you're not satisfying customer needs."[29]
>
> Robert D. Hisrich, Ph.D.

When I was about four, my dad taught me an important marketing principle he learned from Bob Hisrich, the co-author of *Marketing Your Ministry: Ten Critical Principles.*[30]

Give people the choice to say "no" to a few options—yet still say "yes."

You can read this true story (and the lesson) on pages 90-91 of *Mastering the Management Buckets*. Here's how my dad tells it:

Late one afternoon, Jason asked his mom for a cookie.

"No," Joanne said. "It's too close to dinner time."

I took Jason aside and gave him my fatherly advice on effective marketing.

"Here's how to get your cookie, Jason," I began.

"Tomorrow, go into the kitchen and ask Mom this simple question, "Mom? Can I have one cookie or two cookies?"

My street-smart kid learned fast and was patient. The next day he joined his mom in the kitchen and nonchalantly asked, "Mom? Can I have one cookie or two cookies?"

The answer was immediate. "Just one!"

 At PEARPOD, we'll help you serve up a delicious array of choices to the people you serve.

---

[29] John W. Pearson and Robert D. Hisrich, Ph.D., *Marketing Your Ministry: Ten Critical Principles* (Brentwood, TN: Wolgemuth & Hyatt, Publishers, 1990), 98.

[30] Ibid.

6. THE PROGRAM BUCKET

CORE COMPETENCY

We are zealots for program effectiveness and so we research and understand our customer before launching new programs, products or services. We measure program results. We feed our primary programs and drop the losers—all in the spirit of discerning where God is at work.

Strategic Balls in the Program Bucket

❶ GIVE program choices.

❷ BUILD program capacity and sustainability first.

❸ FEED your strongest programs and benchmark the others.

❹ DON'T BE the eighth lemonade stand in a row of nine!

SELF-ASSESSMENT:

☑ **Where is your ORGANIZATION or DEPT. today? What's your 1-year goal?**

	4 LEVELS OF MANAGEMENT KNOWLEDGE AND COMPETENCIES	TODAY	IN 1 YEAR:
Level 1	I don't know what I don't know.		
Level 2	I know what I don't know.		
Level 3	I have an action plan to address what I know I don't know.		
Level 4	I am knowledgeable and effective in this core competency and can mentor others.		

☑ **Where are YOU today? What's your 1-year goal?**

	4 LEVELS OF MANAGEMENT KNOWLEDGE AND COMPETENCIES	TODAY	IN 1 YEAR:
Level 1	I don't know what I don't know.		
Level 2	I know what I don't know.		
Level 3	I have an action plan to address what I know I don't know.		
Level 4	I am knowledgeable and effective in this core competency and can mentor others.		

1 Give Program Choices

When the only two answers are yes or no, you're not satisfying customer needs.

Give people the choice to say
NO
to a few options—
yet still say
YES!

Program Choice Worksheet (1 cookie or 2 cookies?):

PROGRAM, PRODUCT, SERVICE OR DONOR OPTION:	OPTION #1	OPTION #2
1)		
2)		
3)		

P.S. Add "Early Bird" options also!

RESOURCES:

❑ **The Program Bucket: http://managementbuckets.com/program-bucket**
❑ *Marketing Your Ministry: Ten Critical Principles*, by John W. Pearson and Robert D. Hisrich, Ph.D.
❑ TED Talk by Malcolm Gladwell, "Choice, Happiness, and Spaghetti Sauce" - https://www.ted.com/talks/malcolm_gladwell_on_spaghetti_sauce

Build Program Capacity and Sustainability First

You never have a second chance to make a first impression.

Top 10 Questions to Ask About Program Capacity and Sustainability

☑ Check the **3** most important for your organization:

❑ 1. Does this program align with our mission statement?

❑ 2. Does this program align with our Big *Holy* Audacious Goal (BHAG)?

❑ 3. Does this program have written goals that meet the S.M.A.R.T. test (Specific, Measurable, Achievable, Realistic, Time-related)?

❑ 4. Do we have the people capacity to both launch the program and maintain it (a staff champion, support staff, volunteers, etc.)?

❑ 5. Have we answered the five Drucker questions?

❑ 6. Have we invested adequate time and money in researching *Who is the customer?* and *What does the customer value?*

❑ 7. Does this program align with our culture and our core values?

❑ 8. Have we conducted due diligence to assess the program's sustainability (including revenue and expense) over the next three to five years?

❑ 9. Under what conditions do we agree that we will "pull the plug" on this program if the goals are not achieved by the target dates?

❑ 10. Have we been diligent in asking our inside circle for constructive criticism or have we spiritually hyped it so much that naysayers have been silenced?

RESOURCES:

❑ *Nonprofit Sustainability: Making Strategic Decisions for Financial Viability,* by Jeanne Bell, Jan Masaoka and Steve Zimmerman.
❑ *Creators: From Chaucer and Durer to Picasso and Disney,* by Paul Johnson
❑ *Peter Drucker's Five Most Important Questions: Enduring Wisdom for Today's Leaders,* by Peter F. Drucker, Frances Hesselbein, and Joan Snyder Kuhl

③ Feed Your Strongest Programs and Benchmark the Others

All programs are not created equal.

STRATEGIC PROGRAM DEVELOPMENT STANDARD Annual Evaluation of Current & Future Programs Primary Programs & Secondary Programs					
Program Criteria 5 = Currently meets or exceeds criteria 4 = Has met or exceeded criteria at least 2 out of the last 3 years. 3 = Has not met the criteria—but we agree it will likely meet it in the next year. 2 = No reason to believe it will meet the criteria. 1 = Based on this criteria, time to drop it.	**Program A**	**Program B**	**Program C**	**Program D**	**Program E**
1) Program serves a minimum of ___% of our customers (members, donors, etc.)					
2) Program generates a net income of ___%.					
3) The measurable results of this program are improving each year.					
4) Customer research and feedback indicate this program has strong appeal and/or potential.					
5) Let's be honest. This is a "sacred cow" and we'll give it one more year.					
6)					
7)					
TOTAL SCORES:					

Determine score ranges for primary programs and secondary programs.
(Example: Primary programs must score at least 37 out of 50 points.)

RESOURCES:

❑ *Nonprofit Sustainability: Making Strategic Decisions for Financial Viability*, by Jeanne Bell, Jan Masaoka and Steve Zimmerman.
❑ *The Choice: The Christ-Centered Pursuit of Kingdom Outcomes,* by Gary G. Hoag, R. Scott Rodin, and Wesley K. Willmer
❑ *The Nonprofit Strategy Revolution: Real-Time Strategic Planning in a Rapid-Response,* by David La Piana (Note: book gives you access to 27 tools and templates.)

Don't Be the 8th Lemonade Stand in a Row of 9!

It's risky to be the first—it's high risk to be the last.

Marketing Your Ministry
Ten Critical Principles[31]
John W. Pearson and Robert D. Hisrich, Ph.D.

Here are the 10 key points from the book, *Marketing Your Ministry: Ten Critical Principles*, by John Pearson and Robert Hisrich.

☑ **Check the one principle that is most urgent for your organization to address:**

❑ **1.** If you have $10,000 to spend, invest $5,000 in researching and understanding your audience.

❑ **2.** You can't be all things to all people.

❑ **3.** Ask people what their real needs are—then listen, listen, listen.

❑ **4.** If you don't know where you're going, any road will get you there.

❑ **5.** Know your strengths, roll out from them, and then make sure others know them, too.

❑ **6.** Don't be the 8th lemonade stand in a row of 9.

❑ **7.** Don't over-engineer. Your audience won't pay extra for something they cannot appreciate.

❑ **8.** Caution! People are creatures of habit.

❑ **9.** Give people the choice to say "no" to a few options—but still say "yes."

❑ **10.** One clever direct mail piece does not a marketing plan make. People buy a total package.

---

[31] John W. Pearson and Robert D. Hisrich, Ph.D., *Marketing Your Ministry: Ten Critical Principles* (Brentwood, TN: Wolgemuth & Hyatt, Publishers, 1990), 1-115. Note: while this book is currently out of print, some re-sellers offer it on Amazon at: http://amzn.to/2wuUw7O

TO DO OR TO DELEGATE
THE PROGRAM BUCKET

BALL #1: Give Program Choices

Point Person	Task	Deadline	Done!

BALL #2: Build Program Capacity and Sustainability First

Point Person	Task	Deadline	Done!

BALL #3: Feed Your Strongest Programs and Benchmark the Others

Point Person	Task	Deadline	Done!

BALL #4: Don't Be the Eighth Lemonade Stand in a Row of Nine!

Point Person	Task	Deadline	Done!

Bucket Bottom Line:
Research! You get what you pay for. You also get what you research. Launching a new program without researching and understanding your customer, donor or member increases the likelihood for a spectacular program disaster!

SUSTAINABILITY!
Count the Cost

"Is there anyone here who, planning to build a new house, doesn't first sit down and figure the cost so you'll know if you can complete it? If you only get the foundation laid and then run out of money, you're going to look pretty foolish. Everyone passing by will poke fun at you:

'He started something he couldn't finish.'"

Luke 14:28-30 (MSG)

❏ THE CAUSE
☑ **THE COMMUNITY**
❏ THE CORPORATION

Cause, Community, Corporation: The 3-legged Stool

"The buckets in the Community arena are no less important than those of the Cause, but the vocabulary is softer. Here we hone our core competencies in people skills and we seek to create a God-honoring culture with three to five core values. In Community, we build and equip team members and celebrate results using tools from the *Hoopla!* Bucket. We invest time in affirmation . . . not because it increases revenue, but because it honors people.

"Leaders of nonprofit organizations and churches who work with donors and volunteers must balance Cause rhetoric with the warm language of Community—"We are extraordinarily blessed by our volunteers"—and business managers must do the same for their employees, their vendors and their customers."[32]

---

[32] John Pearson, *Mastering the Management Buckets*, 108.

THE COMMUNITY

THE CAUSE
Bucket 1: The Results Bucket
Bucket 2: The Customer Bucket
Bucket 3: The Strategy Bucket
Bucket 4: The Drucker Bucket
Bucket 5: The Book Bucket
Bucket 6: The Program Bucket

THE COMMUNITY
Bucket 7: The People Bucket
Bucket 8: The Culture Bucket
Bucket 9: The Team Bucket
Bucket 10: The *Hoopla!* Bucket
Bucket 11: The Donor Bucket
Bucket 12: The Volunteer Bucket
Bucket 13: The Crisis Bucket

THE CORPORATION
Bucket 14: The Board Bucket
Bucket 15: The Budget Bucket
Bucket 16: The Delegation Bucket
Bucket 17: The Operations Bucket
Bucket 18: The Systems Bucket
Bucket 19: The Printing Bucket
Bucket 20: The Meetings Bucket

#7: THE PEOPLE BUCKET

The chapter on "Dispelling 10 Stereotypical Gender Myths" is worth the price of the book. If you've bought into the myth that women are relationship-oriented and men are task-oriented, you've misread God's unique design in people—male and female. It's a must-read chapter.[33]

COLOR COMMENTARY BY JASON PEARSON

It's human nature for CEOs, senior leaders, marketing team members—even website copywriters—to default to personal preferences. "I think this way. I like this. Everyone else will like this too."

Bad idea!

You must communicate creatively to *all* four social styles:
➢ **Analyticals**
➢ **Drivers**
➢ **Amiables**
➢ **Expressives**

Example: each style has a different approach to decision-making[34]:
- Analyticals avoid risks, based on facts.
- Drivers take risks, based on intuition.
- Amiables avoid risks, based on opinion.
- Expressives takes risks, based on hunches.

One size doesn't' fit all—so you must communicate creatively to all four styles. At PEARPOD, we call the four styles: Info-Sponges, Just-the-Facts, Heartfelts, and Share-Meisters.

Reminder: The most effective pastors, speakers, authors, and website copywriters are those who understand that every sermon and talk must communicate to all four styles. Not easy!

---

[33] Bob Phillips and Kimberly Alyn, *How to Deal With Annoying People: What to Do When You Can't Avoid Them* (Eugene, OR: Harvest House Publishers, 2011), 145-156.
[34] Bob Phillips, *The Delicate Art of Dancing With Porcupines: Learning to Appreciate the Finer Points of Others* (Ventura, CA: Regal, 1989), 50.

7. THE PEOPLE BUCKET

CORE COMPETENCY

We celebrate the God-designed uniqueness of our team members, our customers, our donors, and our volunteers. We are diligent about understanding the four social styles—Analyticals, Drivers, Amiables and Expressives—and helping our people find their comfort zones as they grow in their interpersonal versatility skills.

Strategic Balls in the People Bucket

❶ KNOW your own social style.

❷ COMMUNICATE creatively with the four social styles.

SELF-ASSESSMENT:

☑ **Where is your ORGANIZATION or DEPT. today? What's your 1-year goal?**

	4 LEVELS OF MANAGEMENT KNOWLEDGE AND COMPETENCIES	TODAY	IN 1 YEAR:
Level 1	I don't know what I don't know.		
Level 2	I know what I don't know.		
Level 3	I have an action plan to address what I know I don't know.		
Level 4	I am knowledgeable and effective in this core competency and can mentor others.		

☑ **Where are YOU today? What's your 1-year goal?**

	4 LEVELS OF MANAGEMENT KNOWLEDGE AND COMPETENCIES	TODAY	IN 1 YEAR:
Level 1	I don't know what I don't know.		
Level 2	I know what I don't know.		
Level 3	I have an action plan to address what I know I don't know.		
Level 4	I am knowledgeable and effective in this core competency and can mentor others.		

Know Your Own Social Style

Find your comfort zone and help others feel comfortable.

<u>3 Key Concepts</u>:
- Assertiveness
- Responsiveness
- Versatility

CONTROL

ASK   TELL

EMOTE

THE FOUR SOCIAL STYLES

CONTROL
Tasks/Facts

ANALYTICAL Values Thinking *Withdraws Under Pressure*	**DRIVING** Values Control *Becomes Autocratic Under Pressure*
AMIABLE Values Relationships *Acquiesces Under Pressure*	**EXPRESSIVE** **Values Intuition** *Attacks Under Pressure*

← ASK   TELL →
← SLOW   FAST →

EMOTE
Feelings/Intuition

Social Style Video (5 minutes)
Tracom Group
https://www.youtube.com/watch?v=wRBx8lkV-kQ

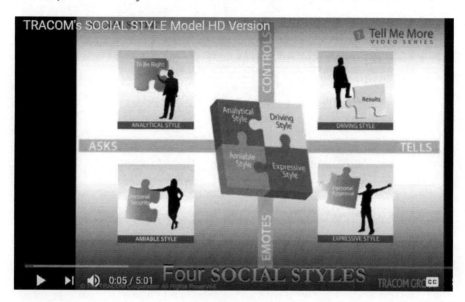

Interpersonal Versatility

Low Versatility	High Versatility
Concerned for self	Concerned for others
Reduces tension for self	Reduces tension for others
Narrow interests	Broad interests
Rigidity	Flexibility
Unwilling to adapt	Adapts
Resistant to feedback	Open to feedback

Do's and Don'ts for the Four Social Styles[35]

Driving	Expressive	Analytical	Amiable
DO	**DO**	**DO**	**DO**
• Speak in terms of concrete results • Focus on the present, the short term • Stick to the point • Do your homework • Stress how the Driver will "win" with your proposition	• Seek ideas, input • Focus on the future • Illustrate concepts with stories • Focus on the big picture • Stimulate their creative impulse • Stress how the Expressive will stand out from the others	• Be logical and well organized • Focus on past, present and future • Give facts, evidence, and lots of data • Focus on detail • Allow time to ponder • Stress how the Analytical can be assured of being right	• Be personal and personable • Focus on tradition • Emphasize a team approach • Be flexible • Allow time to "feel good" • Stress how the Amiable can be "safe"
DON'T	**DON'T**	**DON'T**	**DON'T**
• Be ambiguous • Focus on the long-term • Back down if you're convinced you're right • Give too much detail • Get into a control contest	• Put down the Expressive's enthusiasm and excitement • Be cool and impersonal • Be impatient with side trips and creativity • Be too serious • Give too much detail • Nit-pick	• Rush things • Be intolerant of details • Overlook the past • Be too personal • Be too emotional • Press for immediate action • Appear to not be serious	• Press hard to change things • Push for too much detail • Push for immediate commitment • Be cool and impersonal • Attack • Be dictatorial or autocratic

Back-Against-the-Wall Responses[36]
❑ Analyticals…withdraw.
❑ Drivers…dominate.
❑ Amiables…give in.
❑ Expressives…attack.

---

[35] See endnotes for Chapter 7, The People Bucket, in *Mastering the Management Buckets*.
[36] Bob Phillips, *The Delicate Art of Dancing With Porcupines: Learning to Appreciate the Finer Points of* Others (Ventura, CA: Regal, 1989), 89.

Communicate Creatively

With the Four Social Styles
Just one communication style will fail miserably!

General Overview of the Four Social Styles[37]

	ANALYTICALS	DRIVERS	AMIABLES	EXPRESSIVES
Reaction	Slow	Swift	Unhurried	Rapid
Orientation	Thinking and fact	Action and goal	Relationship and peace	Involvement and intuition
Likes	Organization	To be in charge	Close relationships	Much interaction
Dislikes	Involvement	Inaction	Conflict	To be alone
Maximum effort	To organize	To control	To relate	To involve
Minimum concern	For relationships	For caution in relationships	For affecting change	For routine
Behavior directed toward achievement	PRIMARY EFFORT: Works carefully and alone	PRIMARY EFFORT: Works quickly and alone	SECONDARY EFFORT: Works slowly and with others	SECONDARY EFFORT: Works quickly and with team
Behavior directed toward acceptance	SECONDARY EFFORT: Impress others with precision and knowledge	SECONDARY EFFORT: Impress others with individual effort	PRIMARY EFFORT: Gets along as integral member of group	PRIMARY EFFORT: Gets along as exciting member of group
Actions	Cautious	Decisive	Slow	Impulsive
Skills	Good problem-solving skills	Good administrative skills	Good counseling skills	Good persuasive skills
Decision-making	Avoids risks, based on facts	Takes risks, based on intuition	Avoids risks, based on opinion	Takes risks, based on hunches
Time frame	Historical	Present	Present	Future
Use of time	Slow, deliberate, disciplined	Swift, efficient, impatient	Slow, calm, undisciplined	Rapid, quick, undisciplined

---

[37] Bob Phillips, *The Delicate Art of Dancing With Porcupines: Learning to Appreciate the Finer Points of Others* (Ventura, CA: Regal, 1989), 89.

Chart the Social Styles of Your People
Discover your comfort zone and help the people in your life feel comfortable.

Name	Analytical ✓	Driver ✓	Amiable ✓	Expressive ✓
WORK				
Board Chair:				
Boss/Supervisor:				
Direct Report:				
Direct Report:				
Direct Report:				
Direct Report:				
Direct Report:				
Person who bugs me the most:				
FAMILY				
Spouse:				
Father:				
Mother:				
Children:				
Children:				
Sibling:				
KEY DONORS				
Major Donor				
Major Donor Prospect				

Add: Volunteers, Vendors, Neighbors, Small Group Members, Board Members, etc.

RESOURCES:

❑ **Visit The People Bucket: www.managementbuckets.com/people-bucket**

❑ *The Social Styles Handbook: Find Your Comfort Zone and Make People Feel Comfortable With You*, published by Wilson Learning Library
> Many organizations use the Myers-Briggs Type Indicator, or DISC, or other "personality" type assessments—but few organizations build them thoughtfully into the DNA so CEOs really know their people (by their types) and their board members. The "social styles" system is perhaps the simplest and easiest to remember because the four key words describe the styles: **Driver, Analytical, Amiable and Expressive.**

❑ *How to Deal With Annoying People: What to Do When You Can't Avoid Them*, by Bob Phillips and Kimberly Alyn
> This is the faith-based book on the four social styles, written by Bob Phillips, former executive director of Hume Lake Christian Camps in California. Many consultants find that 80 percent of most conflicts are the result of team members not understanding the basic differences between the four social styles.

❑ Social styles resources (and videos): Tracom Group online at www.socialstyle.com

❑ *The Delicate Art of Dancing With Porcupines: Learning to Appreciate the Finer Points of Others*, by Bob Phillips (out of print, but used copies are available at Amazon.com)

❑ *Versatile Selling: Adapting Your Style So Customers Say Yes!* (Wilson Learning Library)

❑ *Personal Styles & Effective Performance*, by David W. Merrill, Roger H Reid
> This is the original book by the creator of social styles, David W. Merrill.

❑ *7 Seconds to Success: How to Effectively Relate to People in an Instant,* by Gary Coffey and Bob Phillips (4 T's: Thinkers, Tellers, Touchers, Talkers)

❑ *Social Style: The Ah Ha's of Effective Relationships,* by John R. Myers (CEO of Tracom Group) and Gerald L. Prince

---

TO DO OR TO DELEGATE
THE PEOPLE BUCKET

BALL #1: Know your own social style.

Point Person	Task	Deadline	Done!

BALL #2: Communicate creatively with the four social styles.

Point Person	Task	Deadline	Done!

Bucket Bottom Line:
"When it comes to our own behavior, we judge ourselves by our motivations. When it comes to other people's behavior, we judge them by their actions and words."[38]

---

[38] Gary Coffey and Bob Phillips, *7 Seconds to Success: How to Effectively Relate to People in an Instant* (Eugene, OR: Harvest House Publications, 2010), 38.

←SLOWER PACED

6 TIPS ANALYTICAL STYLE
How to Work with Analytical Style People

1. take your **TIME**
2. **COMMUNICATE** clearly & concisely
3. **DON'T PRESSURE** for answers
4. **RESPECT** their processes
5. ask directly for their **FEEDBACK**
6. give them **SPACE**

TRACOM GROUP
THE CREATOR OF **SOCIAL STYLE**®
www.socialstyle.com

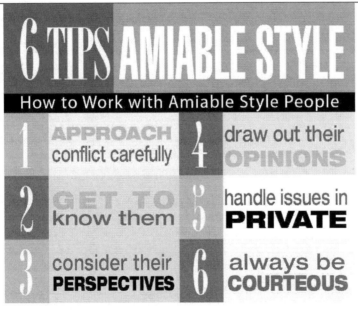

6 TIPS AMIABLE STYLE
How to Work with Amiable Style People

1. **APPROACH** conflict carefully
2. **GET TO** know them
3. consider their **PERSPECTIVES**
4. draw out their **OPINIONS**
5. handle issues in **PRIVATE**
6. always be **COURTEOUS**

TRACOM GROUP
THE CREATOR OF **SOCIAL STYLE**®
www.socialstyle.com

←SLOWER PACED

FASTER PACED→

#8: THE CULTURE BUCKET

Theo Epstein:

"We're not going to compromise character for talent. We're the Cubs. We're going to have both. Talent and character."[39]

COLOR COMMENTARY BY JASON PEARSON:

Have I mentioned that I'm a Cubs fan?

So when "The Culture Bucket" commentary landed on my list, I immediately thought of my favorite MLB team—and how a leader and a manager changed the culture and turned around the losing tradition of the Chicago Cubs.

When Theo Epstein was named president of baseball operations in 2012, he began with culture—and a 259-page spiral-bound road map, "The Cubs Way," the 2012 player development manual. Epstein preached six core principles.[40]

Then Epstein and Manager Joe Maddon made a bet on an "old-school resource: people" and listed their early aspirations:
  • "…maybe we can be better than anyone else with how we treat our players and how we connect with players and the relationships we develop…
  • "Maybe our environment will be the best in the game…
  • "Maybe our vibe will be the best in the game…
  • "Maybe our players will be the loosest and maybe they'll have the most fun…
  • "And maybe they'll care the most."

Did I mention that on Nov. 2, 2016 (my dad's birthday!), the Cubs won the World Series in Game 7?

Go Cubs Go!

---

[39] Tom Verducci, *The Cubs Way: The Zen of Building the Best Team in Baseball and Breaking the Curse* (New York: Crown Archetype, 2017), 76.
[40] Ibid., 100-101.

8. THE CULTURE BUCKET

CORE COMPETENCY

> **We strive to create a corporate culture with core values that are crystal clear.** We yearn for a God-honoring workplace where grace and trust are alive and well. Because we are human we will always have relational conflicts, so we are zealots about resolving conflict early. We invite those who won't live out our values to exit. We experience true joy at work.

Strategic Balls in the Culture Bucket

❶ INVOLVE your team members in defining your culture.

❷ PREACH and live your values.

❸ CUT the cord.

SELF-ASSESSMENT:

☑ **Where is your ORGANIZATION or DEPT. today? What's your 1-year goal?**

	4 LEVELS OF MANAGEMENT KNOWLEDGE AND COMPETENCIES	TODAY	IN 1 YEAR:
Level 1	I don't know what I don't know.		
Level 2	I know what I don't know.		
Level 3	I have an action plan to address what I know I don't know.		
Level 4	I am knowledgeable and effective in this core competency and can mentor others.		

☑ **Where are YOU today? What's your 1-year goal?**

	4 LEVELS OF MANAGEMENT KNOWLEDGE AND COMPETENCIES	TODAY	IN 1 YEAR:
Level 1	I don't know what I don't know.		
Level 2	I know what I don't know.		
Level 3	I have an action plan to address what I know I don't know.		
Level 4	I am knowledgeable and effective in this core competency and can mentor others.		

❶ Involve Your Team Members in Defining Your Culture

When your culture and values are crystal clear, your new people will embrace them with confidence.

Your Corporate Culture - Confidential Assessment

How strongly do you agree or disagree with the following statements?

11 Confidential Questions to Assess Your Culture	1 Strongly Disagree	2 Disagree	3 Neither Agree nor Disagree	4 Agree	5 Strongly Agree
1. The majority of our people are very professional in their work.					
2. Most of the time, we are inappropriately casual at work, and we need to be more professional.					
3. Every team member—no matter his or her title or longevity—is highly valued here.					
4. Having fun at work is a core value for our leaders and managers.					
5. Too often it appears that our programs, products and/or services are more important to us than the people we are serving.					
6. We squander too much time in unnecessary meetings.					
7. Leaders here receive most of the perks and recognition while others "in the trenches" get very little affirmation.					
8. We are diligent about focusing on results and being accountable for results.					
9. Our leaders and managers strive to be God-honoring in their work and in their personal lives.					
10. Based on past experience, when someone has to deliver bad news to a manager, they experience a lot of anxiety about how it will be received.					
11. There seems to be an unhealthy legalism on some issues here, yet other behaviors (gossip and materialism, for example) get a free pass.					
12. If you could add, drop or change just one thing about our corporate culture or core values, what would it be?					

Preach and Live Your Values

Ten core values will never be remembered—much less lived.
Focus on three or four and make them hum!

Pop Quiz!

No.	Do NOT read the instructions in the footnote until your facilitator says "Go!"
I	
II	
III	
IV	
V	
VI	
VII	
VIII	
IX	
X	

Examples of Core Values (add your own):

Read pages 127-130 in *Mastering the Management Buckets*:

U.S. NAVY
H_____
C_____
C_____

AES CORPORATION
To act with _____
To be _____
To have _____
To be socially _____

JOURNEY OF FAITH CHURCH
Welcome
Transform
Serve
http://www.journeyoffaith.com/about-us/about-journey/

Daily Specials

IHOP — Our Values

Integrity: We do the right thing. We are committed to the highest ethical standards.

Excellence: We expect the best from ourselves and each other.

Innovation: We find creative, new ways to delight our guests.

Accountability: We do what we say we will do, we are responsible for our guests.

Inclusion: We respect and value the diversity of others we benefit from many points of view.

Trust: We collaborate and build trust through open, honest communication.

Community: We make a difference in the neighborhoods and communities that we serve.

ASSIGNMENT: the next time you're at IHOP, ask why "tasty food" is not one of their values! Ask team members if they know the values (by memory). Is seven too many?

So you think you can remember up to 10 core values for your organization? Think again! You have five minutes to write down the Ten Commandments (without looking at Exodus 20).

YOUR WEEKLY STAFF MEETING eNews

Issue No. 258 – October 9, 2012
John Pearson, *Editor & Publisher*
http://urgentink.typepad.com/my_weblog/2012/10/make-your-values-mean-something.html

Make Your Values Mean Something

Issue No. 258 of *Your Weekly Staff Meeting* asks you to re-think your core values with a short *HBS* article by Patrick Lencioni on four kinds of values statements.

CORE VALUES FOR DUMMIES

Core values on the wall are routine. Core values lived out—in the boardroom, lunchroom, restroom and choir room—are radical. What's on the wall is often a stunning indicator of what you value most. Let me explain.

Values Statement #1: One quarter in seminary, I took three courses from one of my favorite profs, Elmer Towns. Every weekend he traveled to a megachurch—and after 10 weekends wrote his 1970 classic, *The Ten Largest Sunday Schools and What Makes Them Grow.*

I don't remember the three courses, but I do remember the riveting Monday morning debriefs he shared about his latest ecclesiastical reconnaissance mission. One in particular. Towns told us that one megachurch had an over-sized picture of their pastor on the sanctuary back wall. Huge! The picture next to the founding pastor was Jesus. Much, much smaller.

Values Statement #2: A couple years ago, I visited a mid-size church in Southern California—once known for its choral ministries—and observed that the choir rehearsal room walls were decorated with autographed photos of celebrities, famous musicians and B-list VIPs.

Contrast that signage with the small plaque in the pulpit at the Church of the Open Door in Los Angeles, visible only to the speaker, which read, "Sir, we would see Jesus" (John 12:21).

Values Statement #3: When Lowell Bakke was pastor at Bethany Baptist Church in Puyallup, Wash., the traditional lobby missionary map got a new twist. Under the banner

"Our Missionaries," the map inspired attenders with dozens and dozens of church member snapshots—picturing people in their nine-to-five jobs.

Patrick Lencioni writes, "Most values statements are bland, toothless, or just plain dishonest. And far from being harmless, as some executives assume, they're often highly destructive. Empty values statements create cynical and dispirited employees, alienate customers, and undermine managerial credibility."[41]

Lencioni says there are four categories of values:

☑ **CORE VALUES.** "They are the source of a company's distinctiveness and must be maintained at all costs."

☑ **ASPIRATIONAL VALUES.** These values "are those that a company needs to succeed in the future but currently lacks."

☑ **PERMISSION-TO-PLAY VALUES.** Lencioni says these values, like honesty, integrity and respect for others, are the "minimum behavioral and social standards required of any employee." They don't define or differentiate an organization from others—and should not be considered core values.

For example, one company CEO insisted that integrity was one of their core values. Lencioni cautioned them. "Unless his company was willing to adopt unusually tough measures to demonstrate that it held a higher standard of integrity than most companies, integrity should be classified as a permission-to-play value, not a core value."

☑ **ACCIDENTAL VALUES.** These values "arise spontaneously without being cultivated by leadership and take hold over time." They can be helpful or harmful, such as the accidental value Lencioni discovered at a fashion apparel company where the young, hip employees "owned a disproportionate amount of black clothing."

Yikes! Now what to do with the $3,000 custom-designed graphic of your too-numerous-to-remember values in your office lobby?

Values Statement #4: According to Lencioni, a core value at Siebel is customer satisfaction. "All the artwork on the walls comes from customers' annual reports, and all the conference rooms are named after customers. Even bonuses and compensation packages are awarded on the basis of customer satisfaction surveys conducted by an outside auditor."

What values statements do your walls shout out? Last year I had the privilege of guiding the leadership at Whittier Area Community Church through a core values process. They landed on three: Narration, Exploration, and Celebration. Lencioni would like them!

---

[41] Patrick M. Lencioni, "Make Your Values Mean Something," *Harvard Business Review* (Boston: Harvard Business School Publishing Corporation, July 2002).

Your Weekly Staff Meeting Questions:
1) Pop Quiz! Here's a blank sheet of paper. Write down our core values—word for word. How did you do? Now segment our current values into Lencioni's four categories: Core Values, Aspirational Values, Permission-to-Play Values, and Accidental Values. Any thoughts?

2) When is the last time we affirmed or celebrated a staff member, board member or volunteer who intentionally lived our values? Lencioni says "that employees will not believe a message until they've heard it repeated by executives seven times." What's the next step for us—as a result of having this values statements discussion?

Two options for further study:

❑ **Option 1:** Read or re-read the "How Do We Behave?" section (pages 91 to 104) in Lencioni's best-seller, my 2012 Book-of-the-Year:

The Advantage: *Why Organizational Health Trumps Everything Else in Business,* by Patrick Lencioni

Read my review:
http://urgentink.typepad.com/my_weblog/2012/03/the-advantage.html

❑ **Option 2:** If you'd prefer the "core values for dummies" version, download Lencioni's July 2002 *Harvard Business Review* article, **"Make Your Values Mean Something."** In just four-and-a-half pages, you'll see why cookie-cutter values are boring and inspire no one. You'll also read why Intel "takes pride in the pricklier aspects of its culture" by holding high the values of "engagement confrontation" and "verbal jousting."

TO DO OR TO DELEGATE:

Point Person	Task	Deadline	Done!
	Ask 5 team members to research the core values of at least 5 organizations each.*		

* Discuss the core values of Seattle's Union Gospel Mission

www.ugm.org

✓ **Bold and courageous**
✓ **Diverse brilliance**
✓ **Passionate urgency**
✓ **Strategic effectiveness**
✓ **Pursuit of excellence**
✓ **Sacred trust**
✓ **Innovative and scrappy**

③ Cut the Cord

Have the guts to terminate people who don't live your values.

In their book, *Winning: The Answers—Confronting 74 of the Toughest Questions in Business Today*, Jack and Suzy Welch comment on the "The Ultimate Values Test."[42] They warn not to get rid of value offenders with surreptitious excuses such as, "Charles left for personal reasons to spend more time with his family." Instead, they say, inform your team publicly and "announce that Charles was asked to leave because he didn't adhere to specific company values."

Jack Welch, chairman of GE for 20 years, says that managers should be evaluated on two key areas: their performance and how well they live out the corporate values. This means that, at the end of the day, there are four kinds of managers.

The Ultimate Values Test
Where are your team members today?

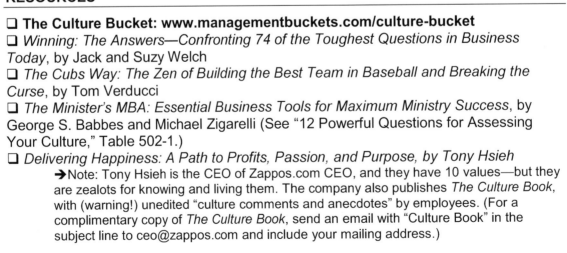

	Lives Our Values	Does NOT Live Our Values
Great Performance	**Group 1:** Praise and reward!	**Group 3:** Warning! Start walking the talk or you're outta here!
Unsatisfactory Performance	**Group 2:** Give them another chance.	**Group 4:** Cut the cord!

RESOURCES

❑ **The Culture Bucket: www.managementbuckets.com/culture-bucket**
❑ *Winning: The Answers—Confronting 74 of the Toughest Questions in Business Today*, by Jack and Suzy Welch
❑ *The Cubs Way: The Zen of Building the Best Team in Baseball and Breaking the Curse*, by Tom Verducci
❑ *The Minister's MBA: Essential Business Tools for Maximum Ministry Success*, by George S. Babbes and Michael Zigarelli (See "12 Powerful Questions for Assessing Your Culture," Table 502-1.)
❑ *Delivering Happiness: A Path to Profits, Passion, and Purpose, by Tony Hsieh*
➔Note: Tony Hsieh is the CEO of Zappos.com CEO, and they have 10 values—but they are zealots for knowing and living them. The company also publishes *The Culture Book*, with (warning!) unedited "culture comments and anecdotes" by employees. (For a complimentary copy of *The Culture Book*, send an email with "Culture Book" in the subject line to ceo@zappos.com and include your mailing address.)

---

[42] Jack and Suzy Welch, *Winning: The Answers—Confronting 74 of the Toughest Questions in Business Today* (New York: HarperCollins, 2006), 57-61.

#9: THE TEAM BUCKET

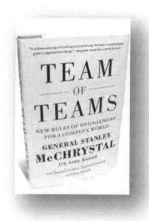

FROM HEROIC LEADER...TO GARDENER!

Are you and your team members facing uphill battles on multiple fronts—fighting the myriad issues noted in the military acronym VUCA…
- volatility
- uncertainty
- complexity
- and ambiguity?

If so, what's your plan?

Gen. Stanley McChrystal has some solutions for you in his book, *Team of Teams.* In his chapter, "Leading Like a Gardener," the general messes with John's favorite movie, *The Hunt for Red October,* starring Sean Connery as Capt. Marko Ramius, the cool-headed CEO of a new Soviet nuclear submarine.

McChrystal says we must reject our love affair with "heroic leaders." Not easy for a four-star general, who led the Joint Special Operations Command in Iraq during the Persian Gulf Wars, and retired in 2010 after serving as commander of all American and coalition forces in Afghanistan. Confessing to his own struggles, he writes: "Although I recognized its necessity, the mental transition from heroic leader to humble gardener was not a comfortable one."[43]

In the chapter recap (three succinct bullet points summarize each chapter), he cautions, "The temptation to lead as a chess master, controlling each move of the organization, must give way to an approach as a gardener, enabling rather than directing."[44]

---

[43] Gen. Stanley McChrystal with Tantum Collins, David Silverman, and Chris Fussell, *Team of Teams: New Rules of Engagement for a Complex World* (New York: Portfolio/Penguin, 2015), 225.
[44] Ibid., 232.

9. THE TEAM BUCKET

CORE COMPETENCY

> **We believe that a balanced life honors God, each other, our families and our friends,** so we leverage the unique set of talents and strengths given to each person by God. Thus we serve with more fulfillment and joy. We also leave work on time, physically and mentally.

Strategic Balls in the Team Bucket

❶ CREATE a time-block culture for your team.

❷ LAMINATE your strengths!

SELF-ASSESSMENT:

☑ **Where is your ORGANIZATION or DEPT. today? What's your 1-year goal?**

	4 LEVELS OF MANAGEMENT KNOWLEDGE AND COMPETENCIES	TODAY	IN 1 YEAR:
Level 1	I don't know what I don't know.		
Level 2	I know what I don't know.		
Level 3	I have an action plan to address what I know I don't know.		
Level 4	I am knowledgeable and effective in this core competency and can mentor others.		

☑ **Where are YOU today? What's your 1-year goal?**

	4 LEVELS OF MANAGEMENT KNOWLEDGE AND COMPETENCIES	TODAY	IN 1 YEAR:
Level 1	I don't know what I don't know.		
Level 2	I know what I don't know.		
Level 3	I have an action plan to address what I know I don't know.		
Level 4	I am knowledgeable and effective in this core competency and can mentor others.		

1 Create a Time-Block Culture for Your Team

Your work will never be done—so go home!

The 21 Time Blocks Toward a God-honoring Balanced Life!

	Sun	Mon	Tues	Wed	Thurs	Fri	Sat
Morning							
Afternoon							
Evening							

AFFIRM

MY AFFIRMATION:

❑ My boss/spouse/family and I agree that on average, 7 out of 8 weeks, I will work a maximum of _____ time blocks per week.
❑ I will have two consecutive days off (6 time blocks) at least every _____ week(s).
❑ I will take compensatory time religiously.
❑ I will take holiday and vacation time religiously.

Signed_____ Date_____

RESOURCES:

❑ **The Team Bucket: www.managementbuckets.com/team-bucket**
❑ *When Work and Family Collide: Keeping Your Job from Cheating Your Family*, by Andy Stanley
❑ *Margin: Restoring Emotional, Physical, Financial, and Time Reserves to Overloaded Lives*, by Richard Swenson, M.D.
❑ *Leading Me: Eight Practices for a Christian Leader's Most Important Assignment*, by Steve A. Brown

From John Pearson's review of *Serve Strong*:
http://urgentink.typepad.com/my_weblog/2016/04/serve-strong.html

Chapter 9, "Captain of the Are Nots," took my breath away. I wrote a big "WOW!" in the margin of page 91. He notes that D.L. Moody, at age 17, was rejected for church membership in Boston and tagged as unable "to fill any extended sphere of public usefulness." The author tagged him, "he was the preeminent are not."[45] (See 1 Cor. 1:26-29.)

---

[45] Terry Powell, *Serve Strong: Biblical Encouragement to Sustain God's Servants* (Abilene, TX: Leafwood Publishers, 2014), 91.

Laminate Your Strengths!

No one has the whole package,
so leverage your Top-5 strengths!

Imagine! What if everyone on your team
received assignments that leveraged their strengths?
"I will praise thee, for I am fearfully and wonderfully made." (Psalm 139:4)

"While the best leaders are not well-rounded, the best teams are."[46]

Strengths Based Leadership:
Great Leaders, Teams and Why People Follow
by Tom Rath and Barry Conchie

According to the Gallup Organization, almost 17 million people worldwide have discovered their CliftonStrengths—their top-five of 34 strengths/talent themes. **Yes…75 percent of the workforce do not leverage their strengths at work every day.** *Yikes!* Instead, many supervisors, bosses and boards focus incorrectly on a leader's weaknesses—instead of his or her strengths.

Each book includes a unique access code for an online assessment at www.gallupstrengthscenter.com. After you complete the 20- to 30-minute online assessment, you will receive a list (and commentary) of your Top-5 strengths. Many teams (and boards) compile these strengths into a chart so that committee assignments and volunteer work are delegated according to a person's strengths. This book includes mini-descriptions of each of the 34 strengths, plus four "case studies" of four CEOs from each of the four major categories of strengths: Executing, Influencing, Relationship Building, and Strategic Thinking.

StrengthsFinder 2.0
Discover Your CliftonStrengths
by Tom Rath

"…our studies indicate that people who do have the opportunity to focus on their strengths every day **are six times as likely** to be engaged in their jobs and more than three times as likely to report having an excellent quality of life in general."

RESOURCES:
❑ Gallup Strengths Center: www.gallupstrengthscenter.com
❑ One-minute YouTube videos of all 34 strengths: www.youtube.com/user/GallupStrengths

---

[46] Tom Rath and Barry Conchie, *Strengths Based Leadership: Great Leaders, Teams and Why People Follow* (New York: Gallup Press, 2008), 2.

Laminate *and Leverage* Your Strengths!
After your team (and board) has completed the StrengthsFinder assessment, prepare wallet-sized laminated cards for each person—as a reminder to "leverage your strengths!"

Option 1:

John Pearson's Top 5 Strengths
1. Focus. You can take a direction, follow through and make the corrections necessary to stay on track. You prioritize, then act.
2. Responsibility. You take psychological ownership of what you say you will do. You are committed to stable values such as honesty and loyalty.
3. Significance. You want to be very important in the eyes of others. You are independent and want to be recognized.
4. Belief. You have certain core values that are unchanging. Out of these values emerges a defined purpose for your life.
5. Maximizer. You focus on strengths as a way to stimulate personal and group excellence. You seek to transform something strong into something superb.

Option 2:

GARY BISHOP – MY STRENGTHS!
RESPONSIBILITY **STRATEGIC** **ACHIEVER** **ARRANGER** **BELIEF**
"I praise you because I am fearfully and wonderfully made; your works are wonderful, I know that full well." Psalm 139:14 (NIV)

Enrich your staff meetings, committee meetings, and board meetings with 8 ½" x 11" (fold in half) tent cards—highlighting the strengths of each person.

OUR TEAM'S Top-5 Strengths from StrengthsFinder.com

Recommendation: color-code this chart.[47]

NAMES➔						
Strength #1						
Strength #2						
Strength #3						
Strength #4						
Strength #5						
EXECUTING						
Achiever						
Arranger						
Belief						
Consistency						
Deliberative						
Discipline						
Focus						
Responsibility						
Restorative						
INFLUENCING						
Activator						
Command						
Communication						
Competition						
Maximizer						
Self-Assurance						
Significance						
Woo						
RELATIONSHIP BUILDING						
Adaptability						
Connectedness						
Developer						
Empathy						
Harmony						
Includer						
Individualization						
Positivity						
Relator						
STRATEGIC THINKING						
Analytical						
Context						
Futuristic						
Ideation						
Input						
Intellection						
Learner						
Strategic						

For more information, visit www.gallupstrengthscenter.com. The "4 Domains of Leadership Strengths" (Executing, Influencing, Relationship Building, and Strategic Thinking) are detailed in the book, *Strengths Based Leadership: Great Leaders, Team and Why People Follow*, by Tom Rath and Barry Conchie. (Chart concept by John Pearson)

---

[47] **Recommendation: color-code this chart.** Email John@JohnPearsonAssociates.com for a color-coded blank template, and a sample completed template that visually shows how "well-rounded" a team is in the four domains.

#10: THE *HOOPLA!* BUCKET

At PEARPOD—and with other teams I've worked with—I'm always looking for creative ways to integrate the *Hoopla!* Bucket with other buckets.

One year I introduced the **Big Red Bowling Ball System** to the creative team during my Silicon Valley days. If the Big Red Bowling Ball was on your desk for too many days, everyone knew that you were the bottleneck on the team's primo project!

The goal: finish your segment of the project and roll the bowling ball over to the team member who was next in line on the task.

The system worked flawlessly. For our end-of-project *Hoopla!* Celebration, instead of awarding a clunky bowling trophy, the team's "most valuable player" was awarded the Big Red Bowling Ball! *Then, we just bought another bowling ball for the next project.*

10. THE *HOOPLA!* BUCKET
CORE COMPETENCY

We harness the power of *hoopla!* for celebration, recreation, intentional food and fellowship gatherings, and just plain fun. We thrive on knock-your-socks-off spontaneity. We believe *hoopla!* honors God. We budget funds for *hoopla!* to mitigate workplace stress and most importantly, to show our team members how much they are loved and appreciated!

Strategic Balls in the *Hoopla!* Bucket

❶ CELEBRATE the appointment of your new international executive vice president of *hoopla!*

❷ LAUNCH your *hoopla!* program with a knock-their-socks-off surprise event!

❸ AFFIRM your team with a F. A. X. (Flipchart Affirmation eXercise)!

❹ RECOGNIZE your team's contributions with spontaneous *hoopla!*

SELF-ASSESSMENT:

☑ **Where is your ORGANIZATION or DEPT. today? What's your 1-year goal?**

	4 LEVELS OF MANAGEMENT KNOWLEDGE AND COMPETENCIES	TODAY	IN 1 YEAR:
Level 1	I don't know what I don't know.		
Level 2	I know what I don't know.		
Level 3	I have an action plan to address what I know I don't know.		
Level 4	I am knowledgeable and effective in this core competency and can mentor others.		

☑ **Where are YOU today? What's your 1-year goal?**

	4 LEVELS OF MANAGEMENT KNOWLEDGE AND COMPETENCIES	TODAY	IN 1 YEAR:
Level 1	I don't know what I don't know.		
Level 2	I know what I don't know.		
Level 3	I have an action plan to address what I know I don't know.		
Level 4	I am knowledgeable and effective in this core competency and can mentor others.		

1 Celebrate the Appointment of Your New International Executive VP of *Hoopla!*

From this moment forth, hoopla! *is a core value.*

H.O.O.P.L.A.	NEXT STEPS:
Honor team members with a year-round *hoopla!* culture.	
Organize *hoopla!* events, parties and celebrations.	
Overwhelm the team with spontaneous fun.	
Pay the *hoopla!* bills from your *hoopla!* budget.	
Laugh a lot—and inspire others to have fun.	
Affirm and appreciate the team with regular doses of *hoopla!*	

Announce the appointment of your Executive VP with (what else...?) *Hoopla!*

Morning email blast	
Bulletin board memo (with balloons!)	
Business cards	
Your idea:	
Your idea:	

RESOURCES

❑ The *Hoopla!* Bucket: www.managementbuckets.com/hoopla-bucket
❑ John Pearson, "*Hoopla!* God Is Honored When We Have Fun!" *Christian Management Report*, Nov. 1999
❑ *The Carrot Principle: How the Best Managers Use Recognition to Engage Their People, Retain Talent, and Accelerate Performance*, by Adrian Gostick and Chester Elton
❑ *Joy at Work: A Revolutionary Approach to Fun on the Job*, by Dennis Bakke

Bucket Bottom Line:
Hoopla! is not what you do, it's a monthly summary of who you are and how much you enjoy working together.

② Launch Your *Hoopla!* Program
With a Knock-Their-Socks-Off Surprise Event!
Make emotional deposits in relational bank accounts.

A cheerful disposition is good for your health;
Gloom and doom leave you bone-tired.
Proverbs 17:22 (MSG)

HOOPLA! IDEAS

1	**Have a Ball at the Mall**
	Congratulations! You now hold in your hot little hands an envelope with cash that must be spent in the next 60 minutes at the mall next door. *You may spend the money only on yourself.* Buy whatever you'd like, except a gift card. Left over cash must be returned to me.
	We'll meet at exactly 2:30 p.m. by the fountain for "Show and Tell." If you're late, you owe me 50 bucks! Ready. Set. Go!
2	
3	
4	
5	

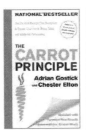

According to *The Carrot Principle*[48], "one-third of the people you give a cash award to will use that money to pay bills. Another one in five won't have any clue in a few months where they spent the money or even how much they received." Think about it: A $50 bonus check makes almost no impression, but a $50 shopping spree with your co-workers is magic. (Note: see Chapter 10 for 125 recognition ideas.)

Bucket Bottom Line:
"Attempt to create the most fun workplace in the world."
Water Cooler Wisdom Rule #3 from *Joy at Work,* by Dennis Bakke[49]

---

[48] Adrian Gostick and Chester Elton, *The Carrot Principle: How the Best Managers Use Recognition to Engage Their People, Retain Talent, and Accelerate Performance* (New York: Free Press, 2007), 9.
[49] www.dennisbakke.com/water-cooler-wisdom

③ Affirm Your Team with a F.A.X.
(Flipchart Affirmation eXercise)!
Write a word or a short phrase of affirmation for each person.

Flipchart Affirmation eXercise (F.A.X.)

Write your affirmations horizontally ➜ but don't affirm yourself!	Affirmations for Dick	Affirmations for George	Affirmations for Luis	Affirmations for Meri	Affirmations for Paul	Affirmations for Toni
DICK		*Deadline-focused*	*Cheerful servant!*	*Super Encourager*	*Incredible Thinker*	*PRAYER WARRIOR*
GEORGE	LOVES US		GENTLE AD-MONISHER	*WOW!*	DETAILED ANALYST	LISTENS TO GOD
LUIS	Thinks the best of us	Organized		Brightens the room!	Busy, but patient.	Random acts of innovation!
MERI	Positive	Lifelong learner	Restorer		REALLY SMART DECISION-MAKER!	faithful and fruitful
PAUL	Woo-er	Balanced discipline	High view of our customers!	Connects our dots with color		Wordsmith
TONI	Heart for God	Goodness	Low ego	Joy, joy, joy, joy, down in her heart!	FAITH!!!!	

"No rules.
Just pray and write from your heart to bless your colleagues."[50]

---

[50] John Pearson, *Mastering the Management Buckets*, 152.

Recognize Your Team's Contributions With Spontaneous *Hoopla!*

Keep your nose to the ground and ask, observe and experiment.

THE RIGHT *HOOPLA!* AT THE RIGHT TIME FOR THE RIGHT REASON!

No.	IDEAS (*Buckets*, pages 153-155)	NEXT STEPS
1	Starbucks gift cards	
2	31 Smiles	
3	Stress Reduction	
4	Elevator Meeting	
5	Time Magazine Person of the Year (2006)	
6	Ban Boring Birthdays	

❑ **7. Sleuth for Success!** *The Carrot Principle* features 125 recognition ideas. Here's Number 34:

"Each day, spend ten minutes looking for someone doing something that furthers your company's goals. When you find it, recognize the person on the spot."[51]

TO DO OR TO DELEGATE:

Point Person	Task	Deadline	Done!

Bucket Bottom Line:
Take fun seriously. The morale, spirit and passion of your team are directly proportional to the amount of time and resources you invest in the *Hoopla! Bucket.*

---

[51] Adrian Gostick and Chester Elton, *The Carrot Principle,* 155.

#11: THE DONOR BUCKET

THE LOW-TRUST PENALTY

Both John and Jason Pearson have been privileged to consult with leading authors, leaders, and CEOs. We help them craft their message and give them pretty blunt feedback (ask them!).

When Jason designs book covers, for example, he knows that this first impression will be a fork-in-the-road: will a reader open the book and experience transformation?

So in reflecting on the Donor Bucket, Jason was so humbled to design the book cover for ECFA President Dan Busby's important book, *TRUST: The Firm Foundation for Kingdom Fruitfulness.*

Busby's wit and quotable quotes are outstanding—and, as you know, if you don't build trust with your donors, you will lose those important relationships. As Busby writes:

"A Christ-centered ministry that lacks trust is like a teenager running through a fireworks factory with a lit blowtorch. It isn't whether something is going to blow up—it's just a matter of when."

"The largest penalty paid by Christ-centered ministries is the 'low-trust' penalty."

For more than 100 quotable quotes on trust from *TRUST*, visit the website.[52]

---

[52] http://www.ecfa.org/trust/QuotableQuotes.aspx

11. THE DONOR BUCKET
CORE COMPETENCY

We believe that extravagant generosity is the biblical norm, not the exception. We challenge donors to give liberally to kingdom causes. We urge prayerful giving to God's work, not for tax benefits nor budget needs. We scrutinize our methodologies not against what works, but against God-honoring principles.

Strategic Balls in the Donor Bucket

❶ UNDERSTAND that fundraising is hard, but transformation is harder.

❷ CREATE a God-honoring development plan.

SELF-ASSESSMENT:

☑ **Where is your ORGANIZATION or DEPT. today? What's your 1-year goal?**

	4 LEVELS OF MANAGEMENT KNOWLEDGE AND COMPETENCIES	TODAY	IN 1 YEAR:
Level 1	I don't know what I don't know.		
Level 2	I know what I don't know.		
Level 3	I have an action plan to address what I know I don't know.		
Level 4	I am knowledgeable and effective in this core competency and can mentor others.		

☑ **Where are YOU today? What's your 1-year goal?**

	4 LEVELS OF MANAGEMENT KNOWLEDGE AND COMPETENCIES	TODAY	IN 1 YEAR:
Level 1	I don't know what I don't know.		
Level 2	I know what I don't know.		
Level 3	I have an action plan to address what I know I don't know.		
Level 4	I am knowledgeable and effective in this core competency and can mentor others.		

① Understand That Fundraising Is Hard, But Transformation Is Harder

Where your treasure is, there your heart will be also.
(Matt. 6:21).

"People go through three conversions:
The conversion of their head, their heart and their pocketbook."
Martin Luther

DISCUSS	NEXT STEPS:
#1. The Treasure Principle	"For where your treasure is, there your heart will be also." (Matt. 6:21 NIV)
#2. The Spiritual Gift of Giving	"…if it is contributing to the needs of others, let him give generously…" (Rom. 12:8 NIV)
#3. Accommodating the Lie for Two-Kingdom Donors[53]	I Chronicles 28 and 29: The Convocation (David and Solomon)
#4. Ben Patterson: "There is no such thing as being right with God and wrong with your money."	

RESOURCES

❑ **The Donor Bucket: www.managementbuckets.com/donor-bucket**
❑ *TRUST: The Firm Foundation for Kingdom Fruitfulness*, by Dan Busby
❑ *The Seven Deadly Sins of Christian Fundraising*, by R. Scott Rodin
❑ *Development 101: Building a Comprehensive Development Program on Biblical Values*, by John R. Frank and R. Scott Rodin
❑ *Ignite Your Generosity: A 21-Day Experience in Stewardship*, by Chris McDaniel
❑ *Revolution in Generosity: Transforming Stewards to Be Rich Toward God*, by Wesley K. Willmer, General Editor
❑ *Giving & Getting in the Kingdom: A Field Guide*, by R. Mark Dillon.
❑ *The Treasure Principle: Unlocking the Secret of Joyful Giving*, by Randy Alcorn
❑ *The Sower: Redefining the Ministry of Raising Kingdom Resources*, by R. Scott Rodin and Gary G. Hoag
❑ *The Third Conversion*, by R. Scott Rodin
❑ *The Guide to Charitable Giving for Churches and Ministries,* by Dan Busby, Michael Martin, and John Van Drunen

---

[53] R. Scott Rodin, *The Seven Deadly Sins of Christian Fundraising* (Colton, WA: Kingdom Life Publishing, 2007), 24.

Create a God-honoring Development Plan

Craft your unique stewardship principles and practices based on prayerful study and research.

In his ground-breaking book, *The Seven Deadly Sins of Christian Fundraising*, Scott Rodin warns us about the extreme danger of living in two kingdoms—God and mammon. He writes:

> "The Christian development office and the local church too often help accommodate this false two-kingdom view. We do it by allowing people to live in this two-kingdom world and never challenging it as unbiblical and soul-destroying. Even worse, we too often develop stewardship programs that operate on these same two-kingdom principles, which means we are not only passively accommodating this distorted view but we are actually supporting it."[54]

The Bible doesn't teach the golf, glitter and gimmicks approach to funding kingdom projects. Paul simply tells Timothy to teach people to be "extravagantly generous" (1 Tim. 6:18).

ASSIGNMENT:

Q1: What is our theology of development?	
Q2: What is the role of the board in development?	
Q3: What is our development strategic plan?	

From John Pearson's review of *Development 101*, by John R. Frank and R. Scott Rodin:

Remarkable! A six-page resource, "An Example of a Theology of Development," is worth the price of the book. (But…really…I could say that about each chapter.)

Olan Hendrix:
"Where there is no vision, the people perish.
Where there is no plan, the vision perishes.
Where there is no money, the plan perishes."

---

[54] R. Scott Rodin, *The Seven Deadly Sins of Christian Fundraising*.

Bonus Ball

Segment Your List and Honor Your Donors!
Understand the continuum from Glorifying God…to Gimmicks.

☑ Simplified segmenting:
Never, ever, ever…send the *same* donor appeal to these two segments:

SEGMENT	DONORS	NON-DONORS
Appeal Purpose	Inspire donor to continue to give.	Inspire person to give a FIRST gift.
Thank You Response	Inspire donor with how her SPECIFIC gift was used.	Welcome! Since this is your first gift, here is additional information about our ministry.
Never, never, never!	Send a generic thank you letter, promoting a project that the donor did not give to.	Thank this person for faithful giving when he has NEVER given!

☑ Advanced segmenting to donors:
What do the donors (customers) value in each of these four segments?

Giving & Getting in the Kingdom: A Field Guide by R. Mark Dillon.

Chapter 4: "The Mind of the Giver"

THE GIFTED GIVER (2-5% of givers) will show up at the dedication of a new building and ask, "What's next?" Dillon says "the gifted giver seldom needs to be asked."

THE THOUGHTFUL GIVER (15-25% of givers) tends to calibrate giving to current income "and rarely involves lowering their net worth to fund what they care about." And, "They have joy in giving, to be sure, but often lack unbridled delight in investing resources for kingdom purposes."

THE CASUAL GIVER (35-50% of givers) "possesses a vague understanding of their obligation to be faithful and generous stewards of their resources, but rarely seek out opportunities to give. They usually give in response to a specific request."

THE RELUCTANT GIVER (perhaps 33% of givers) may be "an overly generous description, because many in this category give very little of their resources for any charitable purpose." Easy to offend, they've had few, if any generosity mentors in their lives. Their parents were unlikely to be kingdom stewards either.

Read John Pearson's review of this book at:
http://urgentink.typepad.com/my_weblog/2012/12/giving-getting-in-the-kingdom.html

The 80/20 Pyramid

DONOR DEVELOPMENT

Major Donors (20%) will give 80%, but most major donors will surface from other donor sources below.

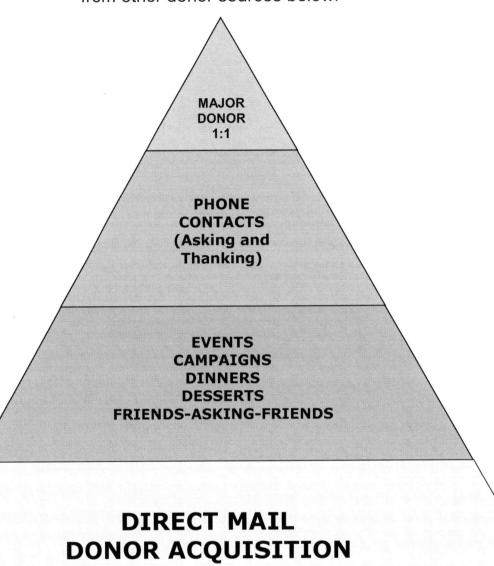

MAJOR
DONOR
1:1

PHONE
CONTACTS
(Asking and
Thanking)

EVENTS
CAMPAIGNS
DINNERS
DESSERTS
FRIENDS-ASKING-FRIENDS

**DIRECT MAIL
DONOR ACQUISITION**

Bonus Ball ④

Just Say Thank You—Again and Again and Again!
Thank donors because it is important—not because it works.

---

7 Ways to Say Thank You:

1. _____

2. _____

3. _____

4. _____

5. _____

6. _____

7. _____

TO DO OR TO DELEGATE:

Point Person	Task	Deadline	Done!

Bucket Bottom Line:
Don't ever think of fundraising the same way again. This is a heart issue and fundraisers will be held responsible for how they communicate Jesus' teaching on stewardship. Heed Scott Rodin's warning to development officers:

**"This is a bad time to get good at doing old things.
The new wine of this biblical way of raising ministry resources
requires new wineskins."[55]**

---

[55] R. Scott Rodin, *The Third Conversion: A Novelette* (Colton, WA: Kingdom Life Publishing, 2011), 90.

How do your organization's fundraising practices compare with ECFA-Accredited organizations?

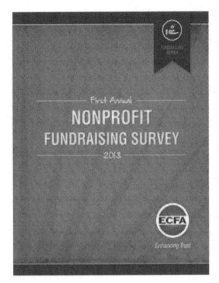 

Download at: www.ecfa.org/Content/Surveys

"Millennials, despite perceptions of their giving patterns, are just as likely as older givers to consider giving via traditional channels. They are less enthusiastic than expected about supporting ministries in the workplace and through social media."[56]

---

[56] *The Generosity Project: Full Report* (Winchester, VA: ECFA Press, 2017), 42.

#12: THE VOLUNTEER BUCKET

COLOR COMMENTARY BY JASON PEARSON:

I'm guessing I was the organization's youngest volunteer, at about age seven, when my dad recruited me to stuff donor envelopes around the dining room table at home.

He would agree—I could fold, insert, lick and stamp envelopes with the best of them!

I have continued to volunteer over the years, but I've also learned how to say no.

My Top-5 strengths in the Gallup StrengthsFinder assessment are: Includer, Maximizer, Strategic, Belief, and Futuristic.

News Flash to All Volunteer Coordinators! When you invite me (and hundreds of other prospects) to volunteer for your worthy cause—leverage my strengths! *Don't think of me as a slot-filler.* Think of me as a person who finds immense fulfillment in serving in volunteer roles that leverage my strengths, my spirituals gifts, my social style (I'm an Amiable), and my passions.

At PEARPOD, we strive to be attentive and intentional about knowing our clients—and helping them leverage their God-given strengths.

Easy? No. But life-changing? *Yes!*

12. THE VOLUNTEER BUCKET

CORE COMPETENCY

We reject the notion of a two-tiered Kingdom workforce. Instead, we seek to treat our paid volunteers (staff) and our unpaid volunteers with equal passion and intentionality. We will never have enough paid staff to accomplish our Kingdom assignments, so we continually hone our skills in volunteer cultivation, recruitment, orientation and engagement.

Strategic Balls in the Volunteer Bucket

❶ BLESS the socks off your volunteers (and walk a mile in their shoes).

❷ ESTABLISH S.M.A.R.T. goals for your volunteer program.

❸ VALUE your volunteers with full organizational support.

❹ CALCULATE the real costs of volunteerism.

SELF-ASSESSMENT:

☑ **Where is your ORGANIZATION or DEPT. today? What's your 1-year goal?**

	4 LEVELS OF MANAGEMENT KNOWLEDGE AND COMPETENCIES	TODAY	IN 1 YEAR:
Level 1	I don't know what I don't know.		
Level 2	I know what I don't know.		
Level 3	I have an action plan to address what I know I don't know.		
Level 4	I am knowledgeable and effective in this core competency and can mentor others.		

☑ **Where are YOU today? What's your 1-year goal?**

	4 LEVELS OF MANAGEMENT KNOWLEDGE AND COMPETENCIES	TODAY	IN 1 YEAR:
Level 1	I don't know what I don't know.		
Level 2	I know what I don't know.		
Level 3	I have an action plan to address what I know I don't know.		
Level 4	I am knowledgeable and effective in this core competency and can mentor others.		

Bless the Socks Off Your Volunteers

(and Walk a Mile in Their Shoes)
Eliminate anything that smacks of second- class status for your unpaid staff.

Read Buckets, pages 167-169	Discussion Thoughts:
Scenario 1: Skipper the Intern	
Scenario 2: Joan of Arkansas	

What's Wrong With This Picture?

- Why do we consistently hire the Skippers of the world when a Joan is patiently waiting in the pew—or in the nursery?

- Why do we impulsively hire paid staff and give inexperienced staff highly responsible assignments but require committed volunteers to work their way up (as if "up" is a biblical concept)?

- Why do we overwork our paid staff, but under-work and under-challenge our unpaid staff?

- Why are the reserved parking places and the anniversary pins allocated to paid staff?

- Why do some churches title their paid staff "pastors" or "directors" while none of their unpaid staff have comparable titles? (Where is that in my Bible?)

- What does payroll have to do with building the kingdom of God?

RESOURCES

❑ **The Volunteer Bucket: www.managementbuckets.com/volunteer-bucket**
❑ *Simply Strategic Volunteers: Empowering People for Ministry,* by Tony Morgan and Tim Stevens
❑ *The Volunteer Revolution: Unleashing the Power of Everybody,* by Bill Hybels

Bucket Bottom Line:
Create a culture that honors paid staff and unpaid volunteers equally. **It's not the paycheck that fosters effectiveness—it's the passion.**

Establish S.M.A.R.T. Goals for Your Volunteer Program

Elevate volunteerism with corporate goals that are Specific, Measurable, Achievable, Realistic and Time-related

The GNOME Chart: Annual Volunteer Goals

Goals	Needs	Objectives	Methods	Evaluation
Goal #1 for **CULTIVATION** is:		1.1 _____ 1.2 _____ 1.3 _____		
Goal #2 for **RECRUITMENT** is:		2.1 _____ 2.2 _____ 2.3 _____		
Goal #3 for **ORIENTATION** is:		3.1 _____ 3.2 _____ 3.3 _____		
Goal #4 for **ENGAGEMENT** is:		4.1 _____ 4.2 _____ 4.3 _____		

Value Your Volunteers

With Full Organizational Support
Enhance volunteer satisfaction and mission results.

The Volunteer Program Annual Check-up

The Seven Strategic Standards of an Effective Volunteer Program	Situational Analysis Today	Where We Want to Be in 12 Months	Next Steps and Ideas
1) We have a written volunteerism philosophy and an annual plan with S.M.A.R.T. goals.			
2) We have a volunteer coordinator who receives continuing training in volunteer management.			
3) We enhance the role of volunteers and ruthlessly eliminate anything in our corporate culture that smacks of second-class status for unpaid staff.			
4) We have one or more volunteer Senior Advisors who we honor publicly with "Dollar-a-Year" recognition (see the Delegation Bucket).			
5) We validate how much we value volunteers by providing superior organizational support in these key areas: ✓ Volunteer budget ✓ Volunteer position descriptions ✓ Volunteer annual calendar of events ✓ Monthly tracking of volunteer hours, achievements and results ✓ Intentional volunteer celebrations, appreciation and *Hoopla!* ✓ Two-way evaluations: (1) Annual evaluations of every volunteer and (2) Volunteer evaluations/feedback on the program and the organization ✓ Newsletters, emails and/or websites, etc., specifically for volunteers			
6) We constantly evaluate the impact and results of our volunteer programs versus employing people to do the same work.			
7) Our board members have clarity on the three hats they wear: the Board Member Hat, the Volunteer Hat and the Participant Hat.[57]			

---

[57] Visit www.ecfa.org/ToolboxSeries.aspx and download the *ECFA Governance Toolbox Series No. 2 - Balancing Board Roles: Understanding the 3 Board Hats: Governance, Volunteer, Participant.*

Calculate the Real Costs of Volunteerism

Establish criteria to determine which jobs should be done by paid volunteers (your staff).

DISCUSSION QUESTIONS:	NEXT STEPS:
#1. What is the real cost of the coffee and donuts?	
#2. Are the right volunteers on the bus?	
#3. Do we have a theological strategy for volunteer/staff recruitment: Are we equipping the saints or paying the saints?	
#4. Are we leveraging each volunteer's spiritual giftedness?	

RESOURCES:

❑ *What You Do Best in the Body of Christ: Discover Your Spiritual Gifts, Personal Style, and God-given Passion*, by Bruce Bugbee
❑ Executive Course in Volunteer Ministry Development: www.newellandassociates.com

TO DO OR TO DELEGATE:

Point Person	Task	Deadline	Done!

Bucket Bottom Line:
"Sustaining motivation is better understood as a by-product as opposed to a goal of itself. It is my experience that if you pursue discipleship with volunteers, motivation will follow. If volunteers see the fulfillment of their role as 'obeying and serving God' rather than serving you or your organization, it will cause motivation to swell."
--Al Newell, High Impact Volunteer Ministry Development - www.newellandassociates.com

#13: THE CRISIS BUCKET

NOT *IF*...BUT *WHEN*.

We help organizations create a climate of trust and grace—so leaders have a safe place to talk shop. In addition to helping clients with their projects, we encourage them to address those critical leadership issues that fester on the back burner.

**It's not *if* a crisis will come—it's *when*.
Are you ready?**

So we deeply appreciate the wisdom in the book, *Judgment: How Winning Leaders Make Great Calls*, by Noel M. Tichy and Warren G. Bennis.[58] A reviewer on Amazon.com called it a "gem among a sea of brain-dead business books."

Judgment, preach the authors, is "the essence of effective leadership." **It involves three domains: people, strategy and crisis.** (Interestingly, those are three of the 20 management buckets: the People Bucket, the Strategy Bucket and the Crisis Bucket.)

They call judgment the proverbial elephant on the table—because it's rarely addressed. "Without a deeper and more compelling understanding of how leaders exercise judgment, the study of leadership can never be complete," they write.

And get this! "Take any leader, a U.S. president, a Fortune 500 CEO, a big league coach, wartime general, you name it. **Chances are you remember them for their best or worst judgment call."** Examples: Harry Truman (atom bomb), Nixon (Watergate), Bill Clinton (Monica), Coca-Cola's Robert Goizueta (New Coke), and Carly Fiorina ("for destroying HP's redoubtable culture").

How will people view your judgment before, during, and after the crisis?

---

[58] Noel M. Tichy and Warren G. Bennis, *Judgment: How Winning Leaders Make Great Calls* (New York: The Penguin Group, 2007), 17.

13. THE CRISIS BUCKET

CORE COMPETENCY

We are prepared for most crises. We have plans in place and a crisis facilitator trained, and we drill our team members frequently and spontaneously. Yet we trust in God, who is our Protector, Comforter and Sustainer.

Strategic Balls in the Crisis Bucket

❶ PLAN now for your next crisis.

❷ DON'T TRUST your instincts in the middle of a crisis.

❸ DRILL, drill and drill again.

SELF-ASSESSMENT:

☑ **Where is your ORGANIZATION or DEPT. today? What's your 1-year goal?**

	4 LEVELS OF MANAGEMENT KNOWLEDGE AND COMPETENCIES	TODAY	IN 1 YEAR:
Level 1	I don't know what I don't know.		
Level 2	I know what I don't know.		
Level 3	I have an action plan to address what I know I don't know.		
Level 4	I am knowledgeable and effective in this core competency and can mentor others.		

☑ **Where are YOU today? What's your 1-year goal?**

	4 LEVELS OF MANAGEMENT KNOWLEDGE AND COMPETENCIES	TODAY	IN 1 YEAR:
Level 1	I don't know what I don't know.		
Level 2	I know what I don't know.		
Level 3	I have an action plan to address what I know I don't know.		
Level 4	I am knowledgeable and effective in this core competency and can mentor others.		

Plan Now for Your Next Crisis

It's not IF you'll have a crisis...but when.

Peter Drucker: "Fortunately or unfortunately, the one predictable thing in any organization is the crisis. That always comes. That's when you do depend on the leader." He said that the job of the leader is to build an organization that is "battle-ready, that has high morale, that knows how to behave, that trusts itself, and where people trust one another."[59]

❑ **Key Principle #1: It's Not If...But When**

Pick Your Crisis...and Discuss:	What would we do?
#1. Radio tower damage	
#2. Moral failure	
#3. Loss of key people	
#4. Ugly terminations	
#5. Unfavorable media report	
#6. Other	

❑ **Key Principle #2: Research Best Practices:**
World Vision's Laminated Card[60]

> **FIVE ESSENTIAL STEPS DURING THE FIRST 24 HOURS FOLLOWING A DISASTER:**
> 1) Activate the National Rapid Response Team
> 2) Send Initial Alert Communication
> 3) Mobilize the Initial Evaluation Process
> 4) Activate Contacts With Donors and Partners
> 5) Mobilize Immediate Response to Affected World Vision Project Zone

YoungLife

> **ACCIDENT/INCIDENT/EMERGENCY 24-HOUR RESPONSE PROCEDURE**
>
> In the event of an accident, incident or emergency in which medical or law enforcement assistance is required to prevent the loss of life or to resolve an unstable or threatening condition in which persons or property appear to be at great risk of injury or damage: 1) Call 9-1-1, and 2) Call the 800 number below.

The card indicates that "this second call will alert a member of YoungLife's crisis response team to the situation you are facing." The instructions also list names to call about insurance and "faith and conduct" issues.

---

[59] Peter F. Drucker with Joseph A. Maciariello, *The Daily Drucker: 366 Days of Insight and Motivation for Getting the Right Things Done* (New York, NY: HarperBusiness, 2004), 112.

[60] Mark Cutshall, "We've Got an Emergency: Essential Lessons Every Manager Needs to Learn Before a Crisis Hits," *Christian Management Report*, August 2005 (San Clemente, CA: Christian Management Association), pp. 7-10. Note: download this article at: www.managementbuckets.com/crisis-bucket

Don't Trust Your Instincts in the Middle of a Crisis

Involve a trusted adviser immediately.

When the hurricane arrives…
and the waters rise…
or adherence to core values plummets…
Do you have a crisis plan?

Tim McDermott, CEO and general manager of Houston's KSBJ Christian radio station, had 18" of water in his own home, but still inspired and encouraged listeners to be the hands and feet of Jesus during the horrific Hurricane Harvey experience in 2017. They had a crisis plan!
http://www.ksbj.org/pages/hope-after-harvey

Blogs and cable news networks have changed the rules for crisis management. If your organization, or one of your people, makes headline news for the wrong reason—how will you respond and how soon? ("No one from the organization responded to our calls or emails.")

Thoughtful leaders plan for crises in advance. They can articulate their message in one sound bite and they have at least one well-trained spokesperson available 24/7 to the media. When you're in crisis mode, it's too late for wordsmithing.

Example: an opinion piece in *The Wall Street Journal* ("The Charity Gap," April 4, 2007) suggested that donors should focus on the poor and redirect giving away from education, health and the arts. So if you're the vice president of advancement and alumni relations at Wheaton College, Wheaton, Ill., how do you respond?

R. Mark Dillon, then Wheaton VP, already had a well-reasoned case statement. His brilliant letter to the editor of *The Wall Street Journal* got top billing in the April 13, 2007, letters section.

The Crisis:	Our Response:
#1. CNN calls our receptionist and asks him for a comment on a negative story that will air in 30 minutes. What are his CEO-approved instructions?	
#2. A well-funded national think tank has labeled your organization as a "hate group." What 3-sentence paragraph will you email to the hostile reporter?	
#3. Your CEO's name is similar to an unrelated person who was just indicated for fraud. Here's a microphone. Give us a 20-second sound bite on how our organization helps society.	

Drill, Drill and Drill Again

Appoint a crisis facilitator and a back-up person.

ASSIGNMENT: Create your own customized crisis response plan:

Our Crisis Plan: _____ Steps

FOUNDATIONAL INFORMATION	NAMES:
This person is our crisis facilitator:	
This person is authorized to speak to the media:	
This person is in charge in the absence of our CEO:	
These people should be notified immediately:	

STEPS:

Step 1	
Step 2	
Step 3	
Step 4	
Step 5	

RESOURCES:
❑ **The Crisis Bucket: www.managementbuckets.com/crisis-bucket**
❑ Google "crisis management"
❑ Ask a wise person, experienced in crisis management, to mentor you.
❑ *Judgment: How Winning Leaders Make Great Calls*, by Noel M. Tichy and Warren G. Bennis
❑ Mark Cutshall, "We've Got an Emergency: Essential Lessons Every Manager Needs to Learn Before a Crisis Hits," *Christian Management Report*, August 2005 (San Clemente, CA: Christian Management Association), pp. 7-10.
❑ Visit: www.store.churchlawtodaystore.com/emergencies.html
❑ *100 Deadly Skills: The SEAL Operative's Guide to Eluding Pursuers, Evading Capture, and Surviving Any Dangerous Situation*, by Clint Emerson, Navy SEAL, Ret.

TO DO OR TO DELEGATE:

Point Person	Task	Deadline	Done!

Bucket Bottom Line:
Don't ever, ever trust your "good judgment" in a time of crisis. Seek professional help.

❑ THE CAUSE
❑ THE COMMUNITY
☑ **THE CORPORATION**

Cause, Community, Corporation: The 3-legged Stool

"When a leader or manager wears the Corporation hat, the focus is on operations, systems, marketing and public relations, boards, and meetings. Here, we give our attention to our fiduciary responsibilities, hiring and firing employees, delegation, organizational charts and budgets.

"The Corporation is not the stuff of the touchy-feely Community arena nor the compelling vision of the Cause—but it's no less important. It takes a delicate of the three arenas to build a sustainable company or organization."[61]

---

[61] John Pearson, *Mastering the Management Buckets*, 190.

THE CORPORATION

THE CAUSE
Bucket 1: The Results Bucket
Bucket 2: The Customer Bucket
Bucket 3: The Strategy Bucket
Bucket 4: The Drucker Bucket
Bucket 5: The Book Bucket
Bucket 6: The Program Bucket

THE COMMUNITY
Bucket 7: The People Bucket
Bucket 8: The Culture Bucket
Bucket 9: The Team Bucket
Bucket 10: The *Hoopla!* Bucket
Bucket 11: The Donor Bucket
Bucket 12: The Volunteer Bucket
Bucket 13: The Crisis Bucket

THE CORPORATION
Bucket 14: The Board Bucket
Bucket 15: The Budget Bucket
Bucket 16: The Delegation Bucket
Bucket 17: The Operations Bucket
Bucket 18: The Systems Bucket
Bucket 19: The Printing Bucket
Bucket 20: The Meetings Bucket

#14: THE BOARD BUCKET

COLOR COMMENTARY BY JASON PEARSON:

I was privileged to design the book cover for the book from Dan Busby and John Pearson, *Lessons From the Nonprofit Boardroom*.

In our creative process, we typically deliver a dozen or more concepts to our clients. The publishing team at ECFAPress selected this sailboat/board table image— and it was our favorite too. *Board service is not for the weak of heart!*

We especially appreciate the first chapter in *Lessons From the Nonprofit Boardroom:*[62]

> Would you trust a surgeon who was not a lifelong learner?
>
> Would you trust an airline pilot who relied on outdated training?
>
> Do your organization's donors and volunteers feel safe in your hands? Why should they trust your ministry's board of directors?
>
> Is your board on top of the rapid changes that are affecting all ministries as well as the changing role of the board?

Those are great questions—and we hope you'll read the answers and insights in the 40 short chapters in *Lessons From the Nonprofit Boardroom.*

---

[62] Dan Busby and John Pearson, *Lessons From the Nonprofit Boardroom* (Winchester, VA: ECFA Press, 2017), 2-3.

14. THE BOARD BUCKET

CORE COMPETENCY

We believe that board members must sense God's call to serve on the board of directors. We invest time in cultivating, recruiting, orienting and engaging board members in their strategic role as stewards of our organization. The first step in organizational sustainability is to inspire board members to be highly committed and generous partners in ministry.

Strategic Balls in the Board Bucket

❶ RECRUIT for passion, not position.

❷ PRAY before prospecting.

❸ DATE before proposing.

❹ INSPIRE your prospect to give generously.

❺ PROPOSE marriage.

❻ CONTINUE dating!

❼ LEAVE a legacy.

SELF-ASSESSMENT:

☑ **Where is your ORGANIZATION or DEPT. today? What's your 1-year goal?**

	4 LEVELS OF MANAGEMENT KNOWLEDGE AND COMPETENCIES	TODAY	IN 1 YEAR:
Level 1	I don't know what I don't know.		
Level 2	I know what I don't know.		
Level 3	I have an action plan to address what I know I don't know.		
Level 4	I am knowledgeable and effective in this core competency and can mentor others.		

☑ **Where are YOU today? What's your 1-year goal?**

	4 LEVELS OF MANAGEMENT KNOWLEDGE AND COMPETENCIES	TODAY	IN 1 YEAR:
Level 1	I don't know what I don't know.		
Level 2	I know what I don't know.		
Level 3	I have an action plan to address what I know I don't know.		
Level 4	I am knowledgeable and effective in this core competency and can mentor others.		

**"A greeter at Wal-Mart gets
more orientation than most board members ever do.**
We all know that's no joke. It's true for boards of every description."

Patrick Lencioni[63]

The 4 Phases of Board Recruitment & Engagement

If you don't plan to engage board members—don't waste your time recruiting them!

❑ 1. Cultivation

❑ 2. Recruitment

❑ 3. Orientation

❑ 4. Engagement

**"I've searched all the parks
in all the cities and found
no statues of committees."**

G.K. Chesterton

---

[63] Jim Brown, *The Imperfect Board Member: Discovering the Seven Disciplines of Governance Excellence* (San Francisco: Jossey-Bass, 2006), xi. (From the foreword by Patrick Lencioni)

Worksheet: The 4 Phases of Board Recruitment & Engagement

☑ In each row, check the box that best describes how effective your board is at these four phases:

THE **4** PHASES OF BOARD RECRUITMENT & ENGAGEMENT	1 VERY INEFFECTIVE	2 INEFFECTIVE	3 NEITHER EFFECTIVE NOR INEFFECTIVE	4 EFFECTIVE	5 VERY EFFECTIVE
1. CULTIVATION • Prayer List • Board Member Criteria • 18 to 36-month plan					
2. RECRUITMENT • Board Nominee Orientation Binder • Board Member Annual Affirmation Statement • Board Roles & Responsibilities • Recruitment Strategy					
3. ORIENTATION • Purposeful New Member Orientation Plan (6 months) • Orientation Feedback Plan					
4. ENGAGEMENT • Preserving and Advancing the Mission • Leveraging the 3 Powerful S's (Strengths, Spiritual Gifts, Social Styles) of Each Member • Customized Annual BHAGs for Each Board Member					

"If board members took an oath of office,
we would first swear to 'preserve and advance the mission of the organization.'
In almost the same breath, we would then pledge to
'accept the responsibility for the election of the CEO
as our solemn duty and sacred trust.'"[64]

---

[64] David L. McKenna, *Stewards of a Sacred Trust: CEO Selection, Transition and Development for Boards of Christ-centered Organizations* (Winchester, VA: ECFA Press, 2010), 17.

7 Steps for Recruiting Board Members:

Excerpted, by permission, from Chapter 14, The Board Bucket, in *Mastering the Management Buckets: 20 Critical Competencies for Leading Your Business or Nonprofit.*[65]

❶ **RECRUIT** for passion—not position.
❷ **PRAY** before prospecting.
❸ **DATE** before proposing!
❹ **INSPIRE** your prospect to give generously.
❺ **PROPOSE** marriage.
❻ **CONTINUE** dating!
❼ **LEAVE** a legacy.

If you work in a large for-profit company, you may not have relationships or influence with your corporate board. But sometime in your career, you'll likely be invited to serve on a church or nonprofit board. This chapter on THE BOARD BUCKET, *the first of seven buckets in the* CORPORATE *arena, is written both for church and nonprofit leaders and their current and prospective board members.*

Peter Drucker said that all boards have one thing in common—they do not function! That may be your experience too. So, while the content of this bucket is focused on the nonprofit world, you'll find excellent resources at the end of this chapter that will be helpful for both for-profit and nonprofit organizations.

* * *

One day way while Jesus was mentoring his disciples, he smiled (tongue-in-cheek) and said, "Show me the money!"

Actually, he said, "Show me your heart." Well…in reality, he said "For where your treasure is, there your heart will be also." (Matthew 6:21 NIV)

As we discussed in THE DONOR BUCKET, this is one of the most profound stewardship principles in Scripture, yet it is rarely practiced where it matters most—with board members of churches and nonprofit Christian organizations.

These arresting words from Jesus would look good on a t-shirt. President Bill Clinton should have said it this way, "It's the heart, stupid!"

The heart issue is the foundational building block for the four stages of building a board: cultivation, recruitment, orientation and engagement.

While there are numerous balls in THE BOARD BUCKET, there are seven key balls—best practices—for recruiting exceptional board members in Christian organizations and churches. It's the first step toward effectiveness and if you ignore or short-cut any of these six steps, you'll pay for it sooner or later. At the end of this chapter, you'll also find a brief list of topics and board resources, if you want to go deeper into this bucket. But first things first. Let's get the right board members on the bus.

 BALL #1:

Recruit for Passion—Not Position.
Invite the already convinced zealots!

Recruit board members for their passion—not their position. Don't swallow the board myth that says you need a CPA, an attorney, a pastor and a fundraiser on your board.

---
[65] John Pearson, *Mastering the Management Buckets*, 191-200.

People in those positions make great volunteers, but might be less-than-loyal, uncommitted board members.

Instead, recruit highly committed people, with board governance skills, who are zealots for your ministry—and have already demonstrated multiple times their high passion for your mission.

If you need a volunteer, recruit a volunteer. If you need a board member, recruit a board member.

 BALL #2:

Pray Before Prospecting
Why settle for second best?

Right now—before you finish this chapter—begin your *Top 50 Prospects Prayer List*. Effective CEOs, senior pastors, and development officers know that it takes up to 36 months to bring exceptional board prospects into the board circle.

Jim Brown, author of *The Imperfect Board Member*, writes, "The problem is, most board cultures are developed by default, not by design."

Change that! The Lord wants you to have an extraordinary board. Imagine the potential when you energize exceptional board members who give spiritual oversight and excellent governance to your God-given mission.

Why settle for second best? Why recruit untested, uncommitted good candidates when—with prayer and hard work—the Lord could bless you with a sterling board team?

 BALL #3:

Date Before Proposing!
Bring board prospects inside the circle of involvement.

Thoughtful adults don't propose marriage on the first date. Effective CEOs don't propose board service to "B List" prospects. Think of this as a 36-month dating experience. But don't mention marriage (board service) up front.

As you pray through the process, slowly bring the prospect inside the circles of involvement. Today, he or she may be unfamiliar with your ministry, so add them to your mailing list and invite them to an event. Test their interest with a volunteer role. Just like in dating, continue to evaluate over many months if your prospect demonstrates growing interest, and ultimately passion, for your important mission.

If Cliff turns out to be a lousy volunteer, drop him! You've saved yourself from marrying a lousy board member. If Susan gives 110 percent and recruits friends and families beyond expectation—you've got a live one! Keep dating!

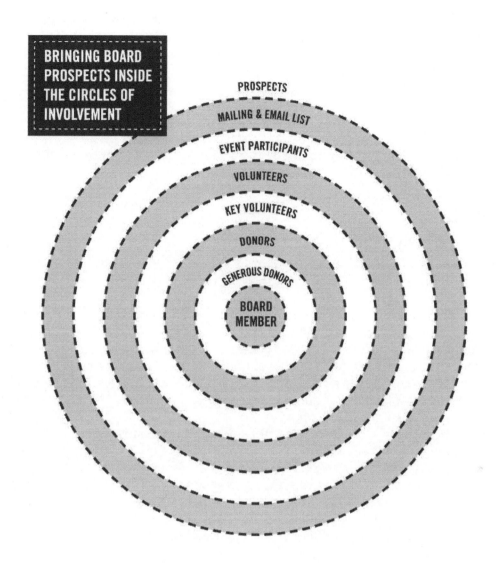

BRINGING BOARD
PROSPECTS INSIDE
THE CIRCLES OF
INVOLVEMENT

PROSPECTS
MAILING & EMAIL LIST
EVENT PARTICIPANTS
VOLUNTEERS
KEY VOLUNTEERS
DONORS
GENEROUS DONORS
BOARD MEMBER

 BALL #4:

Inspire Your Prospect to Give Generously
Model and teach The Treasure Principle.

When you're sharing these principles with other team members and board members, take out Ball #1 in THE DONOR BUCKET and review the principles of generous giving (your heart follows your money). Talk about the biblical values in Randy Alcorn's book, *The Treasure Principle*. The idea of extravagant generosity is not just for board recruitment. It is not a fundraising gimmick. It is a core value for the fully devoted follower of Christ. Don't settle for second best when you're "dating" a board prospect.

Recruit intentionally, with generosity in mind, and you'll breathe new life into your ministry. As you "date" board prospects, challenge them spiritually to become generous givers to your mission. Explain why you need a team of highly committed donors who demonstrate through their giving where their hearts are.

Without waving the carrot of board service (you haven't proposed yet), inspire your prospect (and the spouse, if the person is married) with the opportunity to make your ministry one of their top three annual giving priorities. That's the definition of a generous giver for your ministry.

If a prospect says no, that's OK. You've discovered where his or her heart is— before the wedding. (He or she may already be highly committed, even a generous giver, to two or three other ministries.) That's the good news—you took the temperature on their passion before you popped the question.

Here's the bad news—there are thousands of nonprofit CEOs that have "married" board members way too soon—and the commitment, the passion, the giving and the heart never followed. Save yourself the agony and do it right by starting your prospect prayer list today.

 BALL #5:

Propose Marriage
Once your prospects have moved into the generous giving circle, then it's time to invite them onto the board.

You'll know when it's time to propose marriage (board service). The prospect will have already demonstrated a high level of commitment, all the time moving towards the center of the involvement circle. They will meet all of the previously established board criteria. Plus, the Lord will confirm it to you and your nominating committee.

But again, here's a reminder. Never, never, never invite anyone to serve on your board who is not already a generous giver to your ministry. In my consulting work, I've found I can never say this too many times.

The board candidate does not need to be wealthy—just generous. Generally that means that during this person's term of service on the board, he or she will make your ministry their first, second or third highest annual giving priority. No exceptions. Remember, Jesus said, "For where your treasure is, there your heart will be also."

Where this core value is practiced, board members attest to the remarkable culture change that happens on the board. Passionate, highly committed board members—who follow their money with their heart—become incredible zealots for your mission. Wow!

So when you have prospects that are highly committed to your church or ministry—and meet all the board criteria—pop the question and invite them to serve on your board.

Give them a full ministry briefing, in advance of asking for their decision. Many organizations provide prospects with a Board Nominee Orientation Binder, filled with helpful background information (staff salaries, board minutes, financials—soup to nuts) so the nominee can make an informed and prayerful decision about board service.

Moving Board Donors to Generous Givers
Do you have people on your board today who are not generous givers? Your CEO and/or board chair should plan a one-on-one appointment with each board member. Invite each person to lunch or dinner and mentor your board member on what Jesus taught about giving and why a totally committed board member is so critical. Then ask your board members for their gifts and their hearts.

Worksheet: The Generous Giving Continuum
☑ Check the box that best represents your current board policy on board member giving—and where you'd like it to be in 12 months:

The Generous Giving Continuum	1 We do not believe giving ought to be a criteria for board service.	2 It's the elephant on the table. Our board needs to talk about it—and make a policy decision.	3 We discussed this and have decided NOT to make a board policy on giving.	4 By policy, all board members must be donors of record, but not necessarily at the Top-3 level.	5 By policy, all board members must prioritize their giving to our ministry at the Top-3 level.
Our board's current policy is:					
In 12 months, I'd like to see our policy be:					

**"FOR WHERE YOUR TREASURE IS,
THERE YOUR HEART WILL BE ALSO."**
MATTHEW 6:21 NIV

 BALL #6:

Continue Dating!
Help your board members hone their board governance competencies.

The wedding (board member installation) is only the beginning. Ensure that all board members hone their board competencies regularly. Most will bring a diversity of expectations into your board room. They'll also bring the delightful dysfunctional baggage they've picked up from other board experiences.

Use your board meetings, your conference calls, your mailings and at least one board retreat each year to help members become life-long learners on board best practices. Introduce them to board governance workshops, books, articles, websites and CDs. Invite resource people (consultants, other CEOs, professors, etc.) to train, motivate and inspire your board team. Bless your board members and they'll be a blessing to your ministry!

 BONUS BALL #7:

Leave a Legacy
Grow a great board!

Bob Andringa teaches that one of the greatest legacies a CEO can leave to an organization is a great board. He should know. As managing partner of The Andringa Group (TheAndringaGroup.com) and former president of the Council for Christian Colleges & Universities, Bob has consulted with more than 200 boards over the years. When he speaks or writes books on board governance, nonprofit leaders listen!

A Chinese proverb says that if you want one year of prosperity, grow grain. If you want 10 years of prosperity, grow trees. If you want 100 years of prosperity, grow people.

At this point in your management buckets journey, you may be on overload or just slightly overwhelmed with the CAUSE, COMMUNITY and CORPORATION buckets. You may have a growing list of "I know what I don't know." Don't despair. When you perfect the core competencies in the CORPORATION buckets, you then have the infrastructure for sustainability. Don't neglect THE BOARD BUCKET.

Another Chinese proverb reads, "The best time to plant a tree was twenty years ago. The second best time, is today." Start growing a great board today.

Bucket Bottom Line
When you are effective in THE BOARD BUCKET, it creates a remarkable ripple effect in THE DONOR BUCKET, THE RESULTS BUCKET, and THE VOLUNTEER BUCKET (to name a few). However, when you have low commitment and low passion among board members—and lackluster giving versus extravagant generosity—you will never fully recover and gain organizational momentum until you fix the problems in THE BOARD BUCKET.

BOARD MEETING OR STAFF MEETING? If your nonprofit board of directors meets monthly, your "board" meeting may feel more like a "staff" meeting. Jim Brown says that "the best boards keep their noses in the business and their fingers out!"[66] Frequent board meetings exacerbate the temptation for board members to become too hands-on and the appropriate line between board and staff roles then becomes fuzzy.

While every board culture is unique, many of the most effective nonprofit boards meet quarterly for eight to 12 hours. Some board meetings include an overnight stay with spouses invited for the evening meal. Then telephone conference calls are scheduled in between quarterly meetings, if needed.

[66] Jim Brown, *The Imperfect Board Member*, 88.

RESOURCES:
❏ **The Board Bucket: www.managementbuckets.com/board-bucket**
❏ *The Imperfect Board Member: Discovering the Seven Disciplines of Governing Excellence*, by Jim Brown
❏ *Called to Serve: Creating and Nurturing the Effective Volunteer Board*, by Max De Pree

> Note: John Pearson wrote a series of 25-plus blogs on this book in 2017 for the ECFA blog on Governance of Christ-centered Organizations. Read the first in the series, "Called to Serve: Violence and Committee Meetings."
> http://ecfagovernance.blogspot.com/2017/01/called-to-serve-violence-and-committee.html

❏ *Owning Up: The 14 Questions Every Board Member Needs to Ask,* by Ram Charan
❏ *Stewards of a Sacred Trust: CEO Selection, Transition and Development for Boards of Christ-centered Organizations*, David L. McKenna
❏ *The Nonprofit Board Answer Book: A Practical Guide for Board Members and Chief Executives* (Third Edition) The third edition is based on the first edition, co-authored by Robert C. Andringa and Ted Engstrom.
❏ *Boards That Make A Difference: A New Design for Leadership in Nonprofit and Public Organizations,* by John Carver. Every board member today must understand "policy governance." Carver is the policy governance guru.
❏ *Good Governance for Nonprofits: Developing Principles and Policies for an Effective Board,* by Fredric L. Laughlin and Robert C. Andringa.

New! November 2017

Lessons From the Nonprofit Boardroom
By Dan Busby and John Pearson

40 short chapters—perfect for your "Ten Minutes for Governance" segment in every board meeting.

Order at Amazon and
http://www.ecfa.org/ECFAPress.aspx

TO DO OR TO DELEGATE:

Point Person	Task	Deadline	Done!

Board of Directors: Board Member Orientation Notebook
XYZ ORGANIZATION

	INTRODUCTORY MATERIALS
1	Introduction from the Chairman of the Board of Directors
2	General Brochures, Publications, (eNewsletter, Website outline, etc.)
3	Historical Snapshot, Honors, Awards, Notable News Clippings
	BOARD OF DIRECTORS
4	Current Board Members (Mini-Bios), Committees and Volunteer Structure
5	Board Member Annual Affirmation Statement ❑ Future Board Meetings; Letter of Invitation to Serve; & Bio/Response Form
6	Nomination and Election Procedures
7	Bylaws, Articles of Incorporation, etc.
8	Board Policy Manual
9	Conflict of Interest Disclosure Letter
10	Former Board Members & Board Chairs
11	Board Meeting Agenda/Pages (of most recent meeting) – *sample*
12	Board Issues for Next 3 Years; Skeletons!
	FINANCE, BUDGET, IRS, ECFA REPORTS
13	Annual Budget
14	Current Financial Reports
15	Audited Financial Statements
16	ECFA Membership, Profile and Public Statistics
17	IRS Form 990 *(Return of Org. Exempt from Income Tax)*
	STRATEGIC PLAN & METRICS
18	Strategic Thinking/Planning Process & Strategic Plan Poster (11x17)
19	Annual Satisfaction Surveys
20	CEO Standards of Performance & Board/CEO Accountability Process (Dashboard)
21	Leading Indicators & Key Statistics (charts and graphs)
22	Peter Drucker's "Five Questions Every Nonprofit Organization Must Answer"
23	"Radar Issues" (One-Pager)
	TEAM MEMBERS
24	Organizational Chart & Mini-Position Descriptions: Staff Contact Info
25	Team Member Mini-Bios; CEO Bio, CEO "Strengths"
26	*Confidential Compensation Schedule*
	DEVELOPMENT
27	Donor Development Program - Snapshot
28	Direct Mail, Campaign/Project, Brochure Samples
29	Development Program Annual and Three-year Goals
	PROGRAMS AND SERVICES
30	
31	

#15: THE BUDGET BUCKET

STOP DIGGING!

We wish we had $10 every time we've heard a nonprofit leader whine and push back on sound financial best practices. We often hear:

"But…we're a MINISTRY, not a business!"

The implication, of course, is that "business" practices cannot possibly be God-honoring. *We disagree!*

So be sure to read Bob Buford's counsel to Dan Bolin, a young Christian camp director, in the Budget Bucket chapter. Buford's sage advice to this nonprofit ministry leader: "Don't run out of money!"[67]

Thoughtful budgeting will help you address your sustainability issues. Running out of money will never be God-honoring (read Luke 14:28-30), so don't skip this bucket.

More than once, I've passed along this advice to nonprofit leaders who spent more than they took in:

**"If you find yourself in a hole,
the first thing is to stop diggin'."**

Will Rogers

---

[67] John Pearson, *Mastering the Management Buckets*, 201-202.

15. THE BUDGET BUCKET
CORE COMPETENCY

We operate with integrity and are accountable for best practices in our financial management. We mentor our team members so they understand the financial implications of our programs. We monitor our progress monthly.

Strategic Balls in the Budget Bucket

❶ BUDGET for an annual surplus and a growing reserve.

❷ UNDERSTAND AND COMMUNICATE your cash flow plan.

❸ MONITOR monthly reports.

❹ IMPLEMENT financial best practices.

SELF-ASSESSMENT:

☑ **Where is your ORGANIZATION or DEPT. today? What's your 1-year goal?**

	4 LEVELS OF MANAGEMENT KNOWLEDGE AND COMPETENCIES	TODAY	IN 1 YEAR:
Level 1	I don't know what I don't know.		
Level 2	I know what I don't know.		
Level 3	I have an action plan to address what I know I don't know.		
Level 4	I am knowledgeable and effective in this core competency and can mentor others.		

☑ **Where are YOU today? What's your 1-year goal?**

	4 LEVELS OF MANAGEMENT KNOWLEDGE AND COMPETENCIES	TODAY	IN 1 YEAR:
Level 1	I don't know what I don't know.		
Level 2	I know what I don't know.		
Level 3	I have an action plan to address what I know I don't know.		
Level 4	I am knowledgeable and effective in this core competency and can mentor others.		

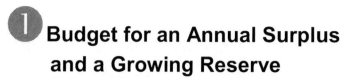

Budget for an Annual Surplus and a Growing Reserve

"Nonprofit" is a tax designation, not a management philosophy.

Since *Mastering the Management Buckets* was written, the U.S. Congress enacted 1,810 public laws between 2007 and 2016.[68] If you are relying on your own instincts or savvy—you will need to read The Crisis Bucket frequently!

1) Create board-approved operating reserves and long-term sustainability goals:

Annual Budget Options

	OPTION A	OPTION B	OPTION C
Annual Revenue	$500,000	$500,000	$500,000
Annual Expense	$475,000	$450,000	$440,000
NET (surplus)	$ 25,000	$ 50,000	$ 60,000
NET = ___% of Annual Revenue	5%	10%	12%

2) Include a SMART Goal in your CEO's annual performance targets:

Standard of Performance
To generate a net surplus of $_____ by the end of the fiscal year.

or:

Standard of Performance
To generate a net surplus of $_____ by the end of the fiscal year toward our goal of growing our cash reserves to $_____ within five years.

---

[68] https://www.govtrack.us/congress/bills/statistics

Understand and Communicate Your Cash Flow Plan

Pumpkin farmers pray,
but they also monitor cash flow forecasts.

Collaborate with your board treasurer to forecast cash flow:

Example: Revenue
(Note: Use the pumpkin farmer example to explain cash flow.)

FY2018 REVENUE	J	F	M	A	M	J	J	A	S	O	N	D	12-Month Total
Revenue Forecast by Month													
Accumulated Revenue Forecast by Month													
Actual Accumulated Revenue Forecast by Month													
Difference (+/-)													

Cash Flow Forecast Monthly Report

	4-Month Forecast	4-Month Actual	Difference
Revenue	$ 135,000	$ 140,000	$ 5,000
Expense	$ 175,000	$ 172,000	$ 3,000
NET	$ (40,000)	$ (32,000)	$ 8,000

"You can sum up this year's budget with one word."

You'll sleep better at night when your organization has cash reserves equal to three to six months of your annual budget.

 **Monitor Monthly Reports**

When you change board treasurers,
don't change your reporting!

Standard Financial Reports

Level 1: Monthly Overview
- ✓ One-page Summary
- ✓ Statement of Activity (Statement of Revenue and Expenses)
- ✓ Statement of Financial Position (Balance Sheet)
- ✓ Statement of Cash Flows

Level 2: Standards of Performance (SMART Goals) Update
- ✓ Leading Indicators (sometimes called "Dashboard Reporting"—progress on key financial goals for the year, including SOPs related to the budget)
- ✓ Cash Flow Graph (12-month cash flow forecast and year-to-date actual)

Level 3: Financial Detail
- ✓ Memo to the Board and Management Team (monthly narrative and notes on highlights, variances and explanations)
- ✓ Appendix (detailed budgets, forecast vs. YTD)

"You start by introducing your topic. Then you say, 'If I were you, I would ask three questions about this topic.' Write the three questions on a flip chart. Answer the three questions. Then stop."[69]

15 Minutes Including Q&A:
A Plan to Save the World From Lousy Presentations
by Joey Asher

REMINDER: Whether you are reporting in person or in writing, remember that you have a diverse audience with diverse needs. In addition, as we learned in the People Bucket, **you are communicating to four social styles: Drivers, Analyticals, Amiables and Expressives**. Each style has preferences, and you need to speak their language if your reports are to be meaningful.

---

[69] Joey Asher, *15 Minutes Including Q&A: A Plan to Save the World From Lousy Presentations* (Atlanta, GA: Persuasive Speaker Press, 2010), 49.

Implement Financial Best Practices

Operate with integrity by becoming a member of ECFA.

ECFA (Evangelical Council for Financial Accountability) has established pass-fail standards of accountability for evangelical Christian organizations and churches. The seven standards also detail best practices that include such topics as the board of directors and audit committee, audited financial statements, use of resources, financial disclosure, conflicts of interest and fundraising.[70]

ECFA-Accredited organizations must affirm their adherence to the *ECFA Seven Standards of Responsible Stewardship.*™ The standards are also an excellent tool for helping your board and staff members move from "I don't know what I don't know" to "I know what I don't know." For example, under the fundraising standards, ECFA members must comply in 11 areas, including truthfulness in communication (donor expectations and intent), incentives and premiums, conflict of interest on royalties, acknowledgement of gifts-in-kind and acting in the interest of the donor.

Is financial accountability important? In 2 Corinthians 8:19-21, the Apostle Paul writes, "[We're] taking every precaution against scandal. We don't want anyone suspecting us of taking one penny of this money for ourselves. We're being as careful in our reputation with the public as in our reputation with God."

When you lead and manage your ministry with integrity—and that integrity is affirmed by an independent organization such as the ECFA—you demonstrate a heart for accountability that honors God, safeguards your staff and board, and provides comfort and confidence to your donors. *Don't be a spiritual Lone Ranger.*

RESOURCES:
❑ **The Budget Bucket: www.managementbuckets.com/budget-bucket**
❑ *2017 Church and Nonprofit Tax & Financial Guide*, by Dan Busby, Michael Martin, and John Van Drunen
❑ *The Guide to Charitable Giving for Churches and Ministries: A Practical Resource on How to Handle Gifts With Integrity*, by Dan Busby, Michael Martin, and John Van Drunen
❑ *Minister's MBA: Essential Business Tools for Maximum Ministry Success*, by George S. Babbes and Michael Zigarelli
❑ *Minding the Money: An Investment Guide for Nonprofit Board Members*, Robert P. Fry, Jr.
❑ Plus: numerous resources to help non-financial staff and board members to better understand financial reports and budgeting: visit BoardSource - ww.boardsource.org

TO DO OR TO DELEGATE:

Point Person	Task	Deadline	Done!

---

[70] ECFA Seven Standards of Responsible Stewardship™ and Commentary - www.ecfa.org/Content/Standards

#16: THE DELEGATION BUCKET

Download all 10 Water Cooler Wisdom posters at:

www.dennisbakke.com/ water-cooler-wisdom

When I suggested to Dennis Bakke that we design "10 Water Cooler Wisdom Posters" as a value-added benefit to his book, *Joy at Work*, I must admit that "Rule #8" got my attention!

RULE #8
Everyone must get advice
before making a decision.
If you don't seek advice,
"you're fired."

Really? Bakke would fire someone who didn't seek advice? What's that about?

Then…when digging deeper into the *Joy at Work* theology and philosophy of going beyond delegation—so other people have joy (not just the leader), it all make sense.

I know. I know. This *Mastering the Management Buckets Workbook* suggests you read a zillion books. (Actually, I'm not even a reader—I'm a listener. I feast on audio books.)

But trust me, *Joy at Work* is one book you must read. Or, if you prefer the business novel genre, read *The Decision Maker,* also by Bakke.

These books will change the way you lead and manage.

LISTENER ALERT!
If you prefer listening versus reading, go to:
www.libro.fm

16. THE DELEGATION BUCKET

CORE COMPETENCY

We are experts at appropriate delegation. We invite team members to accept assignments based on their strengths. We value organized delegation and believe in the Point Person Principle. We track our to-do lists and we add to our don't-do lists.

Strategic Balls in the Delegation Bucket

❶ MENTOR your team on the "monkey" method of delegation.

❷ MAXIMIZE the point person assignment sheet.

❸ DELEGATE your delegation.

❹ RETHINK your delegation assumptions.

❺ DELETE dumb delegation.

❻ BEGIN a Don't-Do list.

SELF-ASSESSMENT:

☑ **Where is your ORGANIZATION or DEPT. today? What's your 1-year goal?**

	4 LEVELS OF MANAGEMENT KNOWLEDGE AND COMPETENCIES	TODAY	IN 1 YEAR:
Level 1	I don't know what I don't know.		
Level 2	I know what I don't know.		
Level 3	I have an action plan to address what I know I don't know.		
Level 4	I am knowledgeable and effective in this core competency and can mentor others.		

☑ **Where are YOU today? What's your 1-year goal?**

	4 LEVELS OF MANAGEMENT KNOWLEDGE AND COMPETENCIES	TODAY	IN 1 YEAR:
Level 1	I don't know what I don't know.		
Level 2	I know what I don't know.		
Level 3	I have an action plan to address what I know I don't know.		
Level 4	I am knowledgeable and effective in this core competency and can mentor others.		

① Mentor Your Team on the "Monkey" Method of Delegation
Get the monkey off your back!

Understand the principles from *The One Minute Manager Meets the Monkey*[71] and mentor your team (and board) with the "monkey" vocabulary.

Rule 1. Describe the Monkey.

Rule 2. Assign the Monkey.

Rule 3. Insure the Monkey, Recommend, Then Act, Act, Then Advise

Rule 4. Check on the Monkey

What's the downside of delegating?

People who ***don't*** take risks
generally make about two big mistakes a year.

People who ***do*** take risks
generally make about two big mistakes a year.
--Peter Drucker

---

[71] Kenneth Blanchard, William Oncken, Jr., and Hal Burrows, *The One Minute Manager Meets the Monkey* (New York: William Morrow and Co., Inc., 1989), 58.

2 Maximize the Point Person Assignment Sheet

This simple tool will revolutionize every meeting.

But first…what are meetings costing you?

Meeting Cost Calculator

Meeting Name: _____

Meeting Date: _____

CONFIDENTIAL

Meeting Participants	Annual Salary and Benefits	Hourly Rate (Divide annual salary and benefits by 2,080 hours.)
1.		$ _____ per hour
2.		$ _____ per hour
3.		$ _____ per hour
4.		$ _____ per hour
5.		$ _____ per hour

Cost of this meeting per hour $ _____

Length of meeting   x _____ hours

Total cost of this meeting   = $ _____

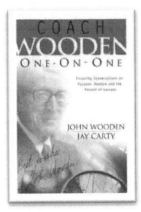

Coach John Wooden on time:

"Time lost is time lost. It's gone forever. Some people tell themselves that they will work twice as hard tomorrow to make up for what they did not do today. People should always do their best. **If they can work twice as hard tomorrow, then they should have also worked twice as hard today.** That would have been their best. Catching up leaves no room for them to do their best tomorrow. People with the philosophy of putting off and then working twice as hard cheat themselves."[72]

---

[72] John Wooden and Jay Carty, *Coach Wooden One-On-One: Inspiring Conversations on Purpose, Passion and the Pursuit of Success* (Ventura, CA: Regal Books, 2003), Day 1.

Maximize the Point Person Assignment Sheet
Project: Vision 2020 Campaign
Project Champion: Julio

Priority A, B, C	Point Person	TASK/ASSIGNMENT Updated on: *July 15 by Julio*	Deadline Date	Done Date
A	Julio	Create campaign master timeline	8/1	
A	Cameron	Recommend SOPs for new position	8/15	
B	Chandler	Submit Draft 1 of the key volunteers list	8/15	
A	Tyler	Showcase 4 concepts for logo and website	8/31	
B	Dick	Propose front-end and back-end research activity	8/31	
C	Olga	Review last campaign and submit Draft 1 budget	9/15	
C	Digger	Recommend *Hoopla!* ideas for campaign celebration	12/15	

ASSIGNMENT: Use the *Point Person Assignment Sheet* to plan a project:

Priority A, B, C	Point Person	TASK/ASSIGNMENT Updated on: _____ by _____	Deadline Date	Done Date

3 Delegate Your Delegation

Small teams require creative delegation.

CREATIVE DELEGATION OPTIONS:	NOTES:
#1. Dollar-a-Year Senior Advisers	
#2. Director of Volunteer Efforts (D.O.V.E)	
#3. Outsource to contractors	
#4. I'll trade you a spreadsheet for a PowerPoint.	
#5. Document the potential of future results.	
#6. Doughnuts and delegation	
#7.	

"You may be seriously overpaid!"

How to Delegate
with Alex Mackenzie
(Audio CD)

Amazon:
http://amzn.to/2eUjELT

Alec Mackenzie, the time management guru, has an *Effective Delegation Quiz* **for you—and if you fail the quiz— he says you may be seriously overpaid!**

TEN DELEGATION QUESTIONS:
1. Do you take work home regularly?
2. Do you work longer hours than your subordinates?
3. Do you spend time doing for others what they could be doing for themselves?
4. When you return from an absence from the office, do you find the in-basket too full?
5. Are you still handling activities and problems you had before your last promotion?
6. Are you often interrupted with queries or requests on on-going projects or assignments?
7. Do you spend time on routine details that others could handle?
8. Do you like to keep a finger in every pie?
9. Do you rush to meet deadlines?
10. Are you unable to keep on top of your priorities?

How many questions were YES?
- ❑ 0 to 1: You are an excellent delegator!
- ❑ 2 to 4: You can improve.
- ❑ 5 to 6: You have a serious delegation problem.
- ❑ 7 to 10: You are undoubtedly doing much of your subordinates' work and may be seriously overpaid!

Read John Pearson's review: http://urgentink.typepad.com/my_weblog/2013/04/how-to-delegate-cd.html

Rethink Your Delegation Assumptions

Have more fun by trusting people to make their delegation decisions.

Joy at Work!

Read *Joy at Work*—and ask your team to discuss this radical approach to work and decision-making.
- It's not consensus.
- It's not delegation.
- It's not empowerment.
- It's giving away all decision-making—but people must rigorously seek advice.[73]

Rule #8:
**Everyone must seek advice
before making a decision.
If you don't seek advice, "You're fired."**

Download
10 Water Cooler Wisdom
posters at:

www.dennisbakke.com/water-cooler-wisdom

What's the big deal about seeking advice? Bakke lists five benefits of the advice-seeking process:

❑ #1. It draws people in: "They become knowledgeable critics or cheerleaders" and "each person whose advice is sought feels honored and needed."
❑ #2. The decision maker learns humility by asking for advice.
❑ #3. It's on-the-job education. "No other form of education or training can match this real-time experience."
❑ #4. The decision-maker is far closer to the issue than senior management. He or she will have to live with their decision.
❑ #5. And finally, "The process is just plain fun for the decision maker because it mirrors the joy found in playing sports."

Note! Read the book to understand the "firing" part.

---

[73] Dennis Bakke, *Joy at Work: A Revolutionary Approach to Fun on the Job* (Seattle: PVG, 2005), 97.

⑤ Delete Dumb Delegation

Do you still need that monthly report?

3-D

List Your Nominees for the 3-D Campaign here:

"I'm on a 90-day **3-D** campaign
to **D**elete **D**umb **D**elegation!"

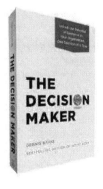

Dennis Bakke preaches a radical approach to decision-making. He says that in a decision-making company:

❑ the leader chooses someone to make a key decision
❑ the decision-maker seeks advice (including from the leader) to gather information
❑ the final decision is made not by the leader, but by the chosen decision-maker.

The Decision Maker: Unlock the Potential of Everyone in Your Organization One Decision at a Time, by Dennis Bakke[74]

---

[74] Dennis Bakke, *The Decision Maker: Unlock the Potential of Everyone in Your Organization One Decision at a Time* (Seattle: Pear Press, 2013)

⑥ Begin a Don't-Do List

If a To-Do list is a $10,000 idea, a Don't-Do list is worth $50,000!

My Don't-Do List

Item No.	Task to STOP Doing	Effective Date	☑ Delete ☑ Ignore ☑ Other	Delegated to:

RESOURCES:

❑ **The Delegation Bucket: www.managementbuckets.com/delegation-bucket**
❑ *The One Minute Manager Meets the Monkey,* by Kenneth H. Blanchard, William Oncken, and Hal Burrows
❑ *Joy at Work,* by Dennis Bakke
❑ The Decision Maker, by Dennis Bakke
❑ *How to Delegate* (Audio CD), with Alec Mackenzie
❑ *Coach Wooden One-On-One: Inspiring Conversations on Purpose, Passion and the Pursuit of Success,* by John Wooden and Jay Carty
❑ Article: "Managing Your Boss" (*Harvard Business Review,* Reprint R0501J – HBR.org)
❑ Article: "Seven Surprises for New CEOs" (*Harvard Business Review,* Reprint R0410C– HBR.org)

TO DO OR TO DELEGATE:

Point Person	Task	Deadline	Done!

Bucket Bottom Line:
Our stewardship of time requires that we understand that time is a gift from God and thus we must make effective use of our team members' time. Effective delegation is all about managing our time. Heed Ephesians 5:15-16 (NASB):
"Therefore be careful how you walk, not as unwise men but as wise, making the most of your time, because the days are evil."

#17: THE OPERATIONS BUCKET

MOTIVATION DOESN'T LAST...

Zig Ziglar said,

"People often say that motivation doesn't last. Well, neither does bathing— that's why we recommend it daily."

So if it's been a very long time since you've coached and mentored your team in the Operations Bucket, here's a reminder that last year's coaching wasn't enough. Don't neglect these five helpful balls in this bucket.

Vision and big ideas are good—but at the end of the day, it's all about execution.

So here's a recent book that will add to your operations repertoire.

Time Management Made (Stupidly) Easy, by Michael R. Clarke, has very practical content including this wake-up call about interruptions—and his solution, the Pomodoro Method.

The author claims "...this one strategy alone has increased my productivity by at least 300%. (And doesn't require a single six-pack of Diet Mountain Dew.)" He's a fan of the Pomodoro Method (google it) because:
 • "The average worker checks their email 30 times an hour."
 • "The average worker checks their smartphone 150 times a day."
 • "The average worker's length of uninterrupted focus is eight minutes."[75]

Wow! Read the book!

---

[75] Michael R. Clarke, *Time Management Made (Stupidly) Easy* (USA: Drive Thru MBA, 2016), 17-18.

17. THE OPERATIONS BUCKET
CORE COMPETENCY

We affirm the high and noble calling of management and the spiritual gift of administration. We reject the fallacy that leaders lead and managers manage. We relentlessly pursue both effective and efficient operational solutions to organizational challenges. We are experts at ruthlessly eliminating costly bureaucracy that impedes results. We are yes men and women!

Strategic Balls in the Operations Bucket

❶ AFFIRM the high and noble calling of management and administration.

❷ SPECIFY "good," "better" or "best."

❸ SHAPE a permission-giving environment.

❹ CLARIFY responsibilities and task ownership.

❺ BLESS Bob with a binder!

SELF-ASSESSMENT:

☑ **Where is your ORGANIZATION or DEPT. today? What's your 1-year goal?**

	4 LEVELS OF MANAGEMENT KNOWLEDGE AND COMPETENCIES	TODAY	IN 1 YEAR:
Level 1	I don't know what I don't know.		
Level 2	I know what I don't know.		
Level 3	I have an action plan to address what I know I don't know.		
Level 4	I am knowledgeable and effective in this core competency and can mentor others.		

☑ **Where are YOU today? What's your 1-year goal?**

	4 LEVELS OF MANAGEMENT KNOWLEDGE AND COMPETENCIES	TODAY	IN 1 YEAR:
Level 1	I don't know what I don't know.		
Level 2	I know what I don't know.		
Level 3	I have an action plan to address what I know I don't know.		
Level 4	I am knowledgeable and effective in this core competency and can mentor others.		

Affirm the high and noble calling of management and administration

Leaders must manage and managers must lead.

Romans 12:6-9, one of the classic texts on spiritual gifts, says in part, "God has given each of us the ability to do certain things well. So if God has given you . . . administrative ability and put you in charge of the work of others, take the responsibility seriously" (*TLB*).

The Bible says that teachers should teach, leaders should lead and **administrators should administer.** It's all about spiritual gift alignment. Yet somehow, the spotlight focuses on leaders and "internationally known speakers" and rarely (if ever) on managers and the gifted team members in operations.

 **Larry Bossidy and Ram Charan write that you get things done with three core processes:[76]**

❑ 1) selecting other leaders
❑ 2) setting the strategic direction
❑ 3) conducting operations.

"Many people regard execution as detail work that's beneath the dignity of a business leader. That's wrong. To the contrary, **it's a leader's most important job.**"

ASSIGNMENT:	Describe the culture in your organization:
Leaders are treated this way➔	
Team members in operations are treated this way➔	

TO DO OR TO DELEGATE:

Point Person	Task	Deadline	Done!

---

[76] Larry Bossidy and Ram Charan, *Execution: The Discipline of Getting Things* Done (New York: Crown Business, 2002), 24.

2 Specify "Good," "Better," or "Best"

Save huge hunks of time with these three clarifying words.

ASSIGNMENT: Read pages 229-230 in *Mastering the Management Buckets* and give an example for a project on your current list.

...at the next weekly staff meeting, I announced a new vocabulary for all future projects: "Good, Better, or Best."

PROJECT NAME:

_____

OPTION	DESCRIPTION	MY PROJECT WOULD LOOK LIKE THIS: ↓
GOOD	If the assignment is for an internal document, the standard might be "Good." Maybe rough calculations on the back of an envelope will be "good enough" for an internal project.	
BETTER	"Better" might require more work because a committee might review it and a "better" job might save us time in the long run.	
BEST	"Best" is reserved when it must be perfect: website copy, donor letters, corporate annual reports, grant applications, etc.	

Always ask: "Should this be Good, Better or Best?"

Notice that the three choices are Good, Better and Best—not Poor, Mediocre and Good-enough-for-church work. Elton Trueblood, the inspirational Quaker author, educator, philosopher, and theologian (1900-1994) wrote,

"Pious shoddy is still shoddy."

❸ Shape a Permission-giving Environment
Ruthlessly eliminate bureaucracy every Friday!

☑ PICK ONE:

BUREAUCRACY-CRUSHER IDEA	OUR PLAN IS TO...
❑ Bagels & Bureaucracy stand-up meeting every Friday.	
❑ **Say "Yes"** by pushing decision-making down. (Read "The Delegation Bucket" chapter.)	
❑ **Delegate!** Ask a team member to read and report on *Getting Things Done: The Art of Stress-free Productivity*, by David Allen, and recommend five ways to create a permission-giving environment.	

BUZZWORD-DU-JOUR. "No software, seminar, cool personal planner, or personal mission statement will simplify your workday or make your choices for you as you move through your day, week, and life. What's more, just when you learn how to enhance your productivity and decision-making at one level, you'll graduate to the next accepted batch of responsibilities and creative goals, whose new challenges will defy the ability of any simple formula or buzzword-du-jour to get you what you want, the way you want to get it."[77]

Bucket Bottom Line:
When Rolla P. Huff was named president and CEO of EarthLink in 2007, the *Wall Street Journal* highlighted his priorities, which underline the importance of the Operations Bucket. Huff said, "It's all about execution. At the end of the day, I won't be judged on my plan as much as my execution."

---

[77] David Allen, *Getting Things Done: The Art of Stress-free Productivity* (New York: Penguin Books, 2001), xii.

Clarify Responsibilities and Task Ownership

Eliminate all fuzzy roles—and identify a point person (or champion) for every task.

Prime Responsibility Chart

P = Prime Responsibility
A = Assistant Responsibility
AP = Approval Required

Tasks and Responsibilities	Board	Executive Committee	CEO	COO	CFO	Program Director
PERSONNEL						
1) Hire and fire the CEO	AP	P				
2) Hire and fire other senior leaders			P			
3) Staff handbook annual review			AP	P	A	
FINANCE & ACCOUNTING						
1) Annual budget	AP		A	A	P	A
2) Quarterly financial reports	AP				P	
3) Annual audit	AP	P			A	
4) Non-budgeted expenditures under $5,000					AP	
STRATEGIC PLAN						
1) Three-year strategic plan update	AP	AP	P	A	A	A
2) Mission, BHAG, core values	AP		P			
3) CEO SOPs	AP	A	P			
Add additional categories below:						

ASSIGNMENT: Discuss the value of using a Prime Responsibility Chart for your overall operations and/or a future project that currently has a fuzzy structure or process. If yes, who will own this? (Who has the monkey?)

5 Bless Bob With a Binder!

A three-ring binder will usher in world peace. Almost.

ASSIGNMENT: What binder is needed first—and who owns this assignment?

☑ We need the following:

- ❑ Operations Binder
- ❑ Baton Binder (hand-off from the person who previously held this position)
- ❑ Vision 2020 Event Binder
- ❑ Employee Benefits Binder
- ❑ Board Member Orientation Binder
- ❑ _____
- ❑ _____
- ❑ _____
- ❑ _____

RESOURCES:

- ❑ **The Operations Bucket: www.managementbuckets.com/operations-bucket**
- ❑ Olan Hendrix, "The Manager Who Leads: Exploring the Unique Qualities of Management and Leadership," *Christian Management Report*, February 2004 (San Clemente, CA: Christian Management Association, 2004), p. 15.
- ❑ *Execution: The Discipline of Getting Things Done*, by Larry Bossidy and Ram Charan
- ❑ *Getting Things Done: The Art of Stress-free Productivity*, by David Allen,
- ❑ The *7 Habits of Highly Effective People*, by Stephen Covey

➔**Where are you investing your best hours of the day, according to Covey's Time Management Matrix? There are four options:**
- ❑ Quadrant 1: urgent and important (crises)
- ❑ Quadrant 2: not urgent and important (planning and preparation);
- ❑ Quadrant 3: urgent and not important (interruptions)
- ❑ Quadrant 4: not urgent and not important (time wasters).

COVEY'S TIME MANAGEMENT MATRIX

	Urgent	Not Urgent
Important	1	2
Not Important	3	4

The goal:
☑ Invest maximum time in Quadrant 2.

TO DO OR TO DELEGATE:

Point Person	Task	Deadline	Done!

#18: THE SYSTEMS BUCKET

I love the poignant story in The Systems Bucket about my Uncle Paul (1939-2015). *Be sure to read the one-page tribute in this section.*

And…like we frequently remind our clients, be sure to prioritize your people over your systems. As Bill Conaty and Ram Charan note in *The Talent Masters: Why Smart Leaders Put People Before Numbers*,

> **"Only one competency lasts.**
> **It is the ability to create a steady,**
> **self-renewing stream of leaders."**[78]

When my Uncle Paul volunteered at a national conference, he leveraged his giftedness in "systems thinking" and mentored a team from the local rescue mission's rehabilitation program. *And he understood that it wasn't about the process—it was about the people.*

I loved what he said to them—after thanking them for their magnificent teamwork:

"When you graduate from your program at the rescue mission, be sure to add this to your resume: Tell future employers that you have experience in process management and that you worked on a just-in-time production assembly line."

Fantastic!

---

[78] Bill Conaty and Ram Charan, *The Talent Masters: Why Smart Leaders Put People Before Numbers* (New York: Crown Business, 2010), 2.

18. THE SYSTEMS BUCKET

CORE COMPETENCY

> **We are passionate about systems thinking and process management.** We encourage systems people to use their gifts and mentor others for the benefit of our Cause and our Community arenas. We are careful not to tinker or over-tweak, yet we are tenacious about tickler systems. We have a heart to create systems that serve people, not the bureaucracy!

Strategic Balls in the Systems Bucket

❶ ADD process management to your résumé.

❷ SEARCH out best practices.

❸ ELIMINATE Tenth-Hole Trash-can Syndrome.

❹ READY! Fire! Aim!

❺ TRAIN your team in tickler tracking.

SELF-ASSESSMENT:

☑ **Where is your ORGANIZATION or DEPT. today? What's your 1-year goal?**

	4 LEVELS OF MANAGEMENT KNOWLEDGE AND COMPETENCIES	TODAY	IN 1 YEAR:
Level 1	I don't know what I don't know.		
Level 2	I know what I don't know.		
Level 3	I have an action plan to address what I know I don't know.		
Level 4	I am knowledgeable and effective in this core competency and can mentor others.		

☑ **Where are YOU today? What's your 1-year goal?**

	4 LEVELS OF MANAGEMENT KNOWLEDGE AND COMPETENCIES	TODAY	IN 1 YEAR:
Level 1	I don't know what I don't know.		
Level 2	I know what I don't know.		
Level 3	I have an action plan to address what I know I don't know.		
Level 4	I am knowledgeable and effective in this core competency and can mentor others.		

On July 17, 2015, this tribute to Paul Pearson (John's oldest brother) was read at a memorial service honoring Paul.

From Chapter 18: The Systems Bucket (p. 236-237)

Mastering the Management Buckets:
20 Critical Competencies for Leading Your Business or Nonprofit
by John Pearson

Add Process Management to Your Resume
Mentor your people to "think systems."

There are genuine experts in your circle who are gifted process managers and systems thinkers.

My brother, Paul, is one of those wonderful MBA types: trained as an engineer, but happiest when serving people in a general manager's role. He has brains and a heart. He's mentored me often through the years, but I still need the brain transplant.

One year at Christian Management Association's annual leadership and management conference in Nashville, Paul volunteered to lead the three-ring binder assembly team. Paul's team members were all in the local rescue mission's rehabilitation program.

On game day, Paul set up the process and the system, assigned the men to the various stations, explained how and why the binders would help managers around the world, and then inspired his men to work as a team. I would have been happy with that. *Not Paul!* He's a fully devoted systems guy.

Thirty minutes into the binder marathon, he stopped the assembly line and held a team meeting. Paul began, "Okay ... now that you see the big picture and your part of the process, what do you recommend we change to make this system run smoother, smarter and simpler?"

The men from rehab, valued people in God's and in Paul's eyes, were at first unprepared for their new consulting roles. But first one and then another made suggestions and, as Paul told me later, they could hardly wait to get back to work to improve the system.

But it didn't stop there. At the end of a fun but physically taxing day, Paul gathered the troops again for his management crème de la crème.

After thanking them for their magnificent teamwork, he added this:
"When you graduate from your program at the rescue mission,
be sure to add this to your resume.
Tell future employers that you have experience in process management
and that you worked on a just-in-time production assembly line."

The broad smiles and high-fives in response reverberated across the room. God smiled, too.

Mentor your people to "think systems." You'll see pure genius ooze out routinely. You'll bless your people and they'll bless you.

Add Process Management to Your Resume

Mentor your people to "think systems."

Systems Bucket: 6 Pointers for Productive Projects

6 STEPS:	PROJECT:
1) Point Person Meet with the previous point person who owned the project last time. Review any files, reports, suggestions, timelines, updates, etc.	
2) Prep Memo Create a briefing memo to prepare for your first team meeting.	
3) Project Tasks & Timeline Create a master list of tasks, assignments and timelines.	
4) Performance Standards What does success look like? Should a Standard of Performance (or SMART Goal) be added to the point person's annual SOPs? What are the leading indicators for this project by key dates? (Revenue, attendance, units sold, donors renewed, etc.)	
5) Party Plan! How will you celebrate success? Who will handle the *hoopla*?	
6) Post-project Evaluation Meeting Build this into your timeline so you have both anecdotal and objective data for next year's project. (You can do an inexpensive survey at SurveyMonkey.com.)	

If you…
don't know what you don't know
in the Systems Bucket,
**…recruit a mentor who is
VERY GOOD at systems!**

② Search Out Best Practices

Study the "E-Myth" systems from the franchising world.

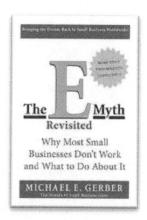

The E-Myth Revisited:
Why Most Small Businesses Don't Work and What to Do About It
by Michael E. Gerber

"Stricken With an Entrepreneurial Seizure"

Nonprofits ministries and churches often get a bad management rap. A popular assumption is that they are poorly managed and have a high failure rate. Hello? Do you read *The Wall Street Journal*? Small businesses fail every day. Ditto the big ones.

According to Michael E. Gerber, 40 percent of all small businesses fail in their first year. Of those that survive one year, 80 percent fail in the next five years. Only 20 percent that make it past five years are around for 10 years. Yikes!

Gerber's insights on business development have stood the test of time. Every organization, he says, should study the principles of franchising. Many nonprofit leaders have built strong organizations by creating great systems (the franchise business model).

Read why technicians who become business owners (entrepreneurs) often miss the key steps for building a business when stricken with an "entrepreneurial seizure" (The E-Myth). It's likely that your organization has content or program experts who are now managing departments or divisions, but still operating as technicians. This book could be a life-saver for them (or you).

DISCUSS:

#1. According to Gerber, 75 percent of franchise businesses are still operating after five years. *Why might that be?*

#2. Franchises use detailed operating manuals, written procedures, and consistent sales approaches. Every detail is delineated. *How would you grade our operations here? Can this place operate for long without the head honchos around? Is there room for improvement?*

TO DO OR TO DELEGATE:

Point Person	Task	Deadline	Done!
	Identify a world-class systems expert and ask this person for their Top-10 list/insights for creating effective systems in your organization.		

③ Eliminate Tenth-Hole Trash-Can Syndrome
Trash distribution is irregular and work never flows evenly in the nine-to-five slot.

ASSIGNMENT: Read The Systems Bucket chapter and then suggest some examples of "Tenth-Hole Trash-Can Syndrome" and your creative remedies.

EXAMPLES	HOW WE WILL FIX THIS:
#1.	
#2.	
#3.	
#4.	
#5.	

RESOURCES:
❑ **The Systems Bucket: www.managementbuckets.com/systems-bucket**
❑ *The E-Myth Revisited: Why Most Small Businesses Don't Work and What to Do About It,* by Michael E. Gerber
❑ *FYI: For Your Improvement: A Guide for Development and Coaching,* by Michael M. Lombardo and Robert W. Eichinger
❑ *The Checklist Manifesto: How to Get Things Right,* by Atul Gawande

TO DO OR TO DELEGATE:

Point Person	Task	Deadline	Done!

Ready! Fire! Aim!

Resist the urge to tinker endlessly to perfect the flawless system. Perfection is not the goal.

ASSIGNMENT: Review the four social styles in The People Bucket and then discern what each style's default approach might be in The Systems Bucket:

SOCIAL STYLE	DEFAULT APPROACH IN THE SYSTEMS BUCKET
Analytical	Ready. Aim. Aim. Aim. Aim. Aim. Aim. Aim…
Driver	
Amiable	
Expressive	

View a video on the four social styles: https://www.youtube.com/watch?v=wRBx8lkV-kQ

 Train Your Team in Tickler Tracking

Track your daily, weekly, monthly, quarterly and annual repeating tasks.

ASSIGNMENT:
Assign one person to use the "D.W.M.Q.A.T. Form" for 30 days and report back on its usefulness for other team members.
Download Worksheet #18.1 at: www.managementbuckets.com/systems-bucket

**Daily-Weekly-Monthly-Quarterly-Annual Tickler Tracking
The "D.W.M.Q.A.T. Form" for Repeatable Tasks**

"I have a Starbucks gift card for the first person who volunteers to try out this form for a month!"

Bucket Bottom Line

The Law of Diminishing Returns fits in many buckets, but it's a frequent sin in the Systems Bucket. Ken Behr cautions leaders and managers to evaluate growth and decline cycles so they know when it's time to pull the plug on a program, product or service. For example, if you invest $5,000 to increase your customer base by 10 percent, should you invest another $5,000—or will you have diminishing returns? If two staff members are overloaded, does adding a third person make economic and organizational sense? Use systems thinking, Behr preaches, to analyze the Law of Diminishing Returns.

#19: THE PRINTING BUCKET

THE MARKETING RULES HAVE CHANGED!

If you lead a nonprofit organization reaching out to churches, does your message get past the receptionist? The No. 10 envelope-with-tickler mail piece will not cut it anymore. (Read the intro to the Printing Bucket chapter.)

Innovators with serious budgets have raised the bar. When Metro-Goldwyn-Mayer Studios, Inc. asked one of Jason's clients to promote the *Rocky Balboa* movie to the faith and family market, everyone understood that a letter, a flyer, and a response device might have worked for the first *Rocky* in 1976 but it would not have the same punch in today's sophisticated world.

Jason's work with clients has helped fuel box office records for *The Passion of the Christ*, *The Chronicles of Narnia*, and *Polar Express*. Yet he knew that *Rocky Balboa* would need even more creativity. So the team created a unique resource box for pastors and youth leaders. The colorful box included a boxing glove, a Rocky t-shirt, a cap, a DVD with video clips, posters and an eight-page *Faith-Based Leader's Resource Guide*—with every element pointing to a content-rich website.

Be assured—the boxing glove made it to the senior pastor's desk. It did not end up in the trash can. The resource box and the eye-catching materials created the platform for serious life-changing decisions.

The bell just rung. It's now Round 10—and the rules have changed for marketing to churches.

19. THE PRINTING BUCKET

CORE COMPETENCY

We elevate the power of the written and spoken word and leverage our communication tools to create synergy and alignment between our mission, BHAG, strategic plans and programs. We believe proofreading and style matters!

Strategic Balls in the Printing Bucket

❶ LEVERAGE your communication tools to keep programs and projects aligned with your BHAG and strategies.

❷ APPOINT and empower a printing coordinator.

❸ CREATE a failsafe proofreading system.

❹ POST your printing deadline calendar by the coffee.

❺ SELECT a style and take off!

❻ MAXIMIZE new technologies and innovations.

SELF-ASSESSMENT:

☑ **Where is your ORGANIZATION or DEPT. today? What's your 1-year goal?**

	4 LEVELS OF MANAGEMENT KNOWLEDGE AND COMPETENCIES	TODAY	IN 1 YEAR:
Level 1	I don't know what I don't know.		
Level 2	I know what I don't know.		
Level 3	I have an action plan to address what I know I don't know.		
Level 4	I am knowledgeable and effective in this core competency and can mentor others.		

☑ **Where are YOU today? What's your 1-year goal?**

	4 LEVELS OF MANAGEMENT KNOWLEDGE AND COMPETENCIES	TODAY	IN 1 YEAR:
Level 1	I don't know what I don't know.		
Level 2	I know what I don't know.		
Level 3	I have an action plan to address what I know I don't know.		
Level 4	I am knowledgeable and effective in this core competency and can mentor others.		

❶ Leverage Your Communication Tools to Keep Programs and Projects Aligned With Your BHAG and Strategies

Use publication deadlines to fine tune organizational decision-making.

ASSIGNMENT: Read the chapter in The Printing Bucket and then discuss these questions with your team members:

QUESTION	ANSWER
#1. Per The Printing Bucket, could we better leverage the "printing" process to make better and quicker decisions?	
#2. If so, how will we "elevate" printing and execution?	
#3. Which team member or department has already figured out how to "elevate" printing and the calendar to make "joy at work" more of a reality?	

TO DO OR TO DELEGATE:

Point Person	Task	Deadline	Done!

Bucket Bottom Line:
"I learned to write to burn the fuzz off my thinking," commented Fred Smith in his pithy book, *Breakfast With Fred.* Use print deadlines to burn the fuzz off your organization's blue sky plans that otherwise would rarely be committed to the printed page (or the website).

② Appoint and Empower a Printing Coordinator

*Your D-Day Dictator will keep your team
on schedule and under budget.*

ASSIGNMENT: Invite your printing coordinator to meet with senior management for 10 minutes—and fill-in-the-blanks to this statement: "I would experience greater joy at work as your printing coordinator if these three things could be improved…"

1.
2.
3.

---

③ Create a Failsafe Proofreading System

Proofreading occurs best after publication!

ASSIGNMENT: Describe your current proofreading system for donor letters, website copy, signage, newsletters, etc. Give it a grade—and then brainstorm three ways to improve proofreading. What are some Proofreading SMART Goals you might set for your chief proofreader? Why is proofreading important?

TYPOS HAPPNE

1.
2.
3.

Post Your Printing Deadline Calendar by the Coffee Maker

Out of sight is out of mind.

ASSIGNMENT: Ask your printer coordinator to visit peers in three to five other organizations and companies—and return with 10 ideas and a plan to implement the best three ideas!

Stephen Wilbers' five keys to great writing will surprise you: Economy, Precision, Action, Music and Personality.

Hum along: "One of the most important things you can do to sharpen your style is to reawaken yourself to the sound of your words, to tune your ears to the rhythm and cadence and flow of your language. It is in this context that you should ask, How can I make this music more pleasing to my readers? What techniques can I learn from accomplished writers? What techniques can I discover on my own?"

RESOURCES:

❑ **The Printing Bucket: www.managementbuckets.com/printing-bucket**
❑ *The Associated Press Stylebook 2017 and Briefing on Media Law,* published by Associated Press
❑ *You've Got to Be Believed to Be Heard: Reach the First Brain to Communicate in Business and in Life,* by Bert Decker
❑ *Keys to Great Writing Revised and Expanded: Mastering the Elements of Composition and Revision (2nd Edition),* by Stephen Wilbers

TO DO OR TO DELEGATE:

Point Person	Task	Deadline	Done!

⑤ Select a Style and Take Off!

Style and spelling matter.

Do we have a style sheet?

❑ **Yes:** Take the rest of today off!
❑ **No:** Meeting dismissed. It's due in the morning!

⑥ Maximize New Technologies and Innovations

Remember! People are readers or listeners.

ASSIGNMENT: Answer these five questions:

QUESTION:	ANSWER:
#1. What's our best example, in the last six months, of leveraging new technologies and innovations in the Printing Bucket?	
Select one of your communication pieces from the last six months that connected to each of the four social styles. (See the Customer Bucket and the People Bucket.)	
#2. Analyticals thought this was perfect:	
#3. Drivers saved time reading this:	
#4. Amiables felt really good about this:	
#5. Expressives enthusiastically told five friends about this:	

When you communicate only from your preferred style, you

miscommunicate to 75 percent of your audience! Effective communication is in the eye and the ear of the customer. **Analyticals** appreciate facts and logic. **Drivers** want short and sweet messages. **Amiables** embrace communiqués that are relationship-rich, while **Expressives** are distracted at the first hint of a boring monologue.

#20: THE MEETINGS BUCKET

COLOR COMMENTARY BY JASON PEARSON:

Jeff Bezos, founder and CEO of Amazon, says:

"BRANDING IS WHAT PEOPLE SAY ABOUT YOU WHEN YOU ARE NOT IN THE ROOM."

So…what would Jeff Bezos say to *you*, when he's *in* your room?

This will surprise you—because he'd start by telling you to be quiet!

Justin Bariso, writing for *Inc.,* said he learned how to do a "silent start" of a meeting from Jeff Bezos. Here's how it works:

"In the opening minutes of some meetings, before any discussion begins, Bezos and his team of senior executives read printed memos [prepared for the meeting] in total silence. The memos have been known to reach up to six pages, and the silent start may last as long as 30 minutes. During this time, moderator and attendees peruse. They scribble notes in the margins.

"But most important, they think," says Bariso.[79]

Whew! That would take guts, right? But we've all endured way-too-many client meetings that accomplished nothing in the first 30 minutes.

My suggestion: read the online article—and customize this insight for your own culture. *Analyticals will love it. Expressives…not so much!*

---

[79] Justin Bariso: "Silent Start: The Brilliant (and Surprising) Meeting Method I Learned From Amazon's Jeff Bezos - Why giving your meetings a 'silent start' can help brilliant ideas emerge." *Inc. Magazine* (posted online on Sept. 18, 2017 at: https://www.inc.com/justin-bariso/amazons-jeff-bezos-uses-a-brilliant-and-surprising.html).

20. THE MEETINGS BUCKET

CORE COMPETENCY

We design meetings like an architect designs buildings. We have high expectations that our purpose-driven meetings will enhance team-building, accountability and our commitment to results. We value Holy Spirit-led meetings. We reject boring meetings.

Strategic Balls in the Meetings Bucket

❶ FOCUS on results with weekly one-on-one meetings.

❷ CREATE a welcoming environment for every meeting.

❸ MAXIMIZE results with four strategic meetings.

SELF-ASSESSMENT:

☑ **Where is your ORGANIZATION or DEPT. today? What's your 1-year goal?**

	4 LEVELS OF MANAGEMENT KNOWLEDGE AND COMPETENCIES	TODAY	IN 1 YEAR:
Level 1	I don't know what I don't know.		
Level 2	I know what I don't know.		
Level 3	I have an action plan to address what I know I don't know.		
Level 4	I am knowledgeable and effective in this core competency and can mentor others.		

☑ **Where are YOU today? What's your 1-year goal?**

	4 LEVELS OF MANAGEMENT KNOWLEDGE AND COMPETENCIES	TODAY	IN 1 YEAR:
Level 1	I don't know what I don't know.		
Level 2	I know what I don't know.		
Level 3	I have an action plan to address what I know I don't know.		
Level 4	I am knowledgeable and effective in this core competency and can mentor others.		

Focus on Results

With Weekly One-on-One Meetings
Invest time in truth-telling and the Top-3 SOPs.

The time and energy invested in weekly one-on-one meetings minimizes miscommunication and maximizes 10 benefits!

10 BENEFITS OF WEEKLY ONE-ON-ONE MEETINGS	NOTES:
❏ 1. Team members are **affirmed** regularly.	
❏ 2. Direct reports more consistently **leverage their strengths**, their social styles and their spiritual gifts.	
❏ 3. **Standards of performance** (SMART Goals) are clear and goals are achieved on time and under budget.	
❏ 4. Staff conflict, gossip and misinformation challenges are dramatically reduced because **truth-telling** is a practiced core value.	
❏ 5. **Bottlenecks** and missed deadlines are eliminated.	
❏ 6. Recommendations are more thoughtful and **intentional**.	
❏ 7. **Communication is enhanced** as you use your direct report's preferred communication style.	
❏ 8. The **pulse** (morale, passion and energy) of your team is checked weekly.	
❏ 9. Affirmed and productive team members mean **less staff turnover**.	
❏ 10. **And . . . team members often give you affirmation!**	

RESOURCES:
❏ **The Meetings Bucket: www.managementbuckets.com/meetings-bucket**
❏ Download the two-page template, "Weekly Update to My Supervisor" and the "Commentary" on how to use template: www.managementbuckets.com/meetings-bucket

Weekly Update to My Supervisor (Page 1 of 2)

Email or hand deliver this update to your supervisor each week by <u>Tuesday 4 p.m.</u>, in preparation for your one-on-one meeting each Wednesday.

DATE: _____

TO: _____   **FROM:** _____

1. My Snapshot:

My Top 5 Strengths From: *StrengthsFinder 2.0*	1 2 3 4 5
My Social Style From: *The Social Styles Handbook and www.socialstyle.com*	[ ] Analytical [ ] Driver [ ] Amiable [ ] Expressive
My Top 3 Spiritual Gifts From: *Discover Your Spiritual Gifts*	[ ] _____ [ ] _____ [ ] _____
My Learning Preference	I am a: [ ] Reader [ ] Listener

2. My Supervisor's Snapshot

Top 5 Strengths	1 2 3 4 5
Social Style	[ ] Analytical [ ] Driver [ ] Amiable [ ] Expressive
Top 3 Spiritual Gifts	1 _____ 2 _____ 3 _____
Learning Preference	My supervisor is a: [ ] Reader [ ] Listener

3. Here's the status of my *Job Success Tools:*

Current: Yes or No	Job Success Tools	Date Approved
Yes\No	Position Description	
Yes\No	Annual Standards of Performance *(SOPs/SMART Goals)*	
Yes\No	Annual Professional Development Plan *(The 3 C's)*	
Yes\No	To Do List (A, B and C Priorities)	
Yes\No	Tickler Tracker (Daily/Weekly/Monthly/Quarterly/Annually Repeating Tasks)	

4. Last week, I made progress on the following:

_____

_____

5. This week, I am focusing on:

_____

_____

Weekly Update to My Supervisor (Page 2 of 2)

6. Before I make my decision, I need your advice on:

_____

7. The monkey's on your back! I'm waiting on you for:

_____

8. I am recommending that:

_____

9. FYI! You should be aware of the following:

_____

10. Overall, I am:
[ ] OK   [ ] Great!   [ ] Never been better
[ ] Overwhelmed   [ ] Overloaded for the next _____ days
[ ] Don't cancel our meeting! We need to talk!
[ ] Help! I need more time with you. At least _____ hours in the next _____ days.
[ ] Other: _____

11. Our next meetings are scheduled for:

Date	Day	Time	Major Agenda Item(s)

12. I continue to affirm our core value on "Truth-Telling." To my knowledge, I have not shared anything inappropriate with others about you (or another staff person) that I have not shared first with you (or the other person). And, to my knowledge, when others have shared something about you (or others) with me that may be "crossing the line," I have stopped them in their tracks—and reminded them about our core values—and urged them to share it with you (or that person) within 48 hours.

This past week, our working relationship has been:
    [ ] Excellent   [ ] Great   [ ] OK   [ ] Could Be Better   [ ] Poor
    [ ] You blessed me when you _____
    [ ] You bugged me when you _____
    [ ] I need _____ minutes with you to go into the "Tunnel of Chaos."

13. My Top 3 Standards of Performance/SMART Goals *(These remain the same all year.)*
Here are my 3 Most Strategic SOPs (S.M.A.R.T. Goals) that were approved by _____ on _____. I understand that the successful accomplishment of these SOPs is our primary focus in our weekly and quarterly meetings. They will account for about _____% towards my annual evaluation and future compensation adjustments. (Consequently, this weekly update focuses primarily on these three SOPs and their critical importance to the mission and goals of our organization.)

1.

2.

3.

NOTE: This Word™ Document is located at www.managementbuckets.com/meetings-bucket under "The Meetings Bucket." Customize this template for your own use so the basic information remains the same each week.
[Internal Bureaucracy #98765, Rev. Sept. 2017 by GWB]

2 Create a Welcoming Environment for Every Meeting

The meeting begins when the first person arrives.

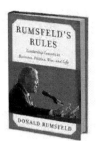

Rumsfeld's Rules (400 of them!):

"The act of calling a meeting about a problem can in some cases be confused with actually doing something."

"As drill sergeants are fond of saying, 'If you're five minutes early, you're on time. If you're on time, you're late. If you're late, you have some explaining to do.'"

"The first consideration for meetings is whether to call one at all."[80]

W.O.W. Factor Meeting Evaluation Form

☑ **W**elcoming
☑ **O**rganized
☑ **W**arm

Evaluation of _____ Meeting

Submitted by _____ Date _____

Rate the WOW Factor for each item below on a scale of 1 to 5.
1 = Utter failure!
2 = Did NOT meet expectations
3 = Met some expectations
4 = Met expectations
5 = Exceeded expectations

WELCOMING

_____ Meeting room was ready 15 minutes before start time.
_____ Meeting facilitator was prepared and relaxed, ready to greet the first person who arrived.
_____ Meeting participants were encouraged to get acquainted and converse with each other.
_____ Guests or new participants were welcomed into the pre-meeting circles of conversation.

(continued on next page)

---

[80] Donald Rumsfeld, *Rumsfeld's Rules: Leadership Lessons in Business, Politics, War, and Life* (New York: HarperCollins, 2013), 27, 31, 303.

W.O.W. Factor Meeting Evaluation Form (continued)

ORGANIZED

_____ The agenda, meeting purpose and anticipated outcomes of the meeting were distributed at least 1 to 7 days in advance of the meeting to every participant.

_____ The meeting agenda was distributed or posted on a flipchart, whiteboard or PowerPoint.

_____ The agenda included a time budget for each topic.

_____ The presenters were well-prepared and any materials distributed were helpful.

_____ The assignments and next steps were agreed upon.

_____ The meeting ended 5 minutes early.

WARM

_____ Food and beverage presentation (if provided) was appropriate.

_____ Prayer (if included) was meaningful and not routine.

_____ Room temperature was acceptable.

_____ Facilitator demonstrated warmth and wisdom in leading the meeting.

_____ Participants demonstrated warmth and wisdom and engaged in the meeting.

_____ Meeting room environment enhanced the meeting (tidiness, extra chairs removed, adequate lighting).

RESOURCES:

❑ **The Meetings Bucket: www.managementbuckets.com/meetings-bucket**

❑ *Read This Before Our Next Meeting: The Modern Meeting Standard for Successful Organizations*, by Al Pittampalli

❑ *The Secret to a Good Meeting Is the Meeting Before the Meeting: Lesson 18 from Leadership Gold* (Kindle Edition), by John C. Maxwell

TO DO OR TO DELEGATE:

Point Person	Task	Deadline	Done!

Bucket Bottom Line:
☑ "If you can't have the meeting before the meeting, don't have the meeting.
☑ "If you do have the meeting before the meeting, but it doesn't go well, don't have the meeting.
☑ "If you have the meeting before the meeting and it goes as well as you hoped, then have the meeting!"[81]

---

[81] John C. Maxwell, *Leadership Gold: Lessons I've Learned from a Lifetime of Leading* (Nashville, Thomas Nelson, 2008), 170. (Note: Each chapter, including Chapter 18, "The Secret to a Good Meeting..." is also available as a Kindle book on Amazon for $1.99 as of Sept. 2017.)

③ Maximize Results With 4 Strategic Meetings

Follow Patrick Lencioni's pattern for four kinds of meetings with your team.

Patrick Lencioni's Four Types of Meetings:
A Leadership Fable...about solving the most painful problem in business

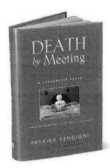

The Real Cost of Bad Meetings!

According to an article in *Spirit Magazine*, the Patrick Lencioni "argues that **bad meetings lead to poor decision-making,** which ultimately creates mediocrity in organizations. In addition, Lencioni says that bad meetings not only exact a toll on the attendees as they suffer through them, but **also cause real human anguish in the form of anger, lethargy, and cynicism**, and even in the form of lower self-esteem."

ASSIGNMENT: Read the book (or download the template) and fill-in the remaining two columns on the four types of meetings every team should have:

MEETING TYPE	TIME REQUIRED	PURPOSE AND FORMAT	TIPS
Daily Check-in	5 to 10 minutes		
Weekly Tactical	45 to 90 minutes		
Monthly Strategic	2 to 4 hours		
Quarterly Off-site Review	1 to 2 days		

➔**Download a two-page description** of the four types of meetings that Patrick Lencioni urges every team to utilize: www.tablegroup.com/imo/media/doc/death_by_meeting2.pdf

RESOURCES:
❏ *Death by Meeting: A Leadership Fable . . . About Solving the Most Painful Problem in Business,* Patrick Lencioni
❏ More resources from Patrick Lencioni at The Table Group – www.TableGroup.com

TO DO OR TO DELEGATE:

Point Person	Task	Deadline	Done!

☑ COMMITMENT
TO LIFELONG LEARNING

☑ My Top-3 Buckets

☑ My Top Take-Away

☑ Online Tools, Templates, and Worksheets

☑ Master List of John Pearson's Book Reviews

☑ About the Authors

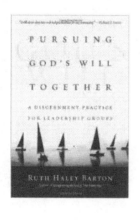

Ruth Haley Barton:

**"Just because something is strategic
does not necessarily mean
it is God's will for us right now."**[82]

---

[82] Ruth Haley Barton, *Pursuing God's Will Together: A Discernment Practice for Leadership Groups* (Downers Grove, IL: InterVarsity Press, 2012), 99.

MY TOP-3 BUCKETS

ASSIGNMENT: After completing your study of all 20 buckets/core competencies, assess your strengths in each of the buckets—and then identify your Top-3. How will you communicate your giftedness in these three buckets to your supervisor, your colleagues, and your direct reports?

CAUSE	COMMUNITY	CORPORATION
❏ 1. The Results Bucket	❏ 7. The People Bucket	❏ 14. The Board Bucket
❏ 2. The Customer Bucket	❏ 8. The Culture Bucket	❏ 15. The Budget Bucket
❏ 3. The Strategy Bucket	❏ 9. The Team Bucket	❏ 16. The Delegation Bucket
❏ 4. The Drucker Bucket	❏ 10. The *Hoopla!* Bucket	❏ 17. The Operations Bucket
❏ 5. The Book Bucket	❏ 11. The Donor Bucket	❏ 18. The Systems Bucket
❏ 6. The Program Bucket	❏ 12. The Volunteer Bucket	❏ 19. The Printing Bucket
	❏ 13. The Crisis Bucket	❏ 20. The Meetings Bucket

MY TOP-3 BUCKETS:	MY STRENGTHS IN THIS BUCKET INCLUDE:
No. ___ _____ Bucket	☑ ☑ ☑ ☑ ☑
No. ___ _____ Bucket	☑ ☑ ☑ ☑ ☑
No. ___ _____ Bucket	☑ ☑ ☑ ☑ ☑

MY
TOP
TAKE-AWAY

ASSIGNMENT: What is your Number One Top Take-Away from your study and discussion of the 20 management buckets?

MY TOP TAKE-AWAY IS:

[blank box]

TO CEMENT THE LEARNING, I WILL SHARE THIS WITH:

[blank box]

AND WHAT ELSE?

Michael Bungay Stanier says the best coaching question in the world is the AWE question: **"And What Else?"**[83]

In a four-minute drill with another board chair, I was instructed to ask four questions displayed on the seminar room screen. Stanier says "the first answer someone gives you is almost never the only answer, and it's rarely the best answer," so the AWE question is the perfect follow-up.

- ✓ Q1: What's the real challenge here for you?
- ✓ Q2: And what else?
- ✓ Q3: And what else?
- ✓ Q4: So what's the real challenge here for you?

---

[83] Michael Bungay Stanier, *The Coaching Habit: Say Less, Ask More & Change the Way You Lead Forever* (Toronto: Box of Crayons Press, 2016), 12.

MY TOP-20 TASKS

To-Do List

NO.	TASK	DEADLINE DATE	DONE DATE
1			
2			
3			
4			
5			
6			
7			
8			
9			
10			
11			
12			
13			
14			
15			
16			
17			
18			
19			
20			

ACCOUNTABILITY PLAN:

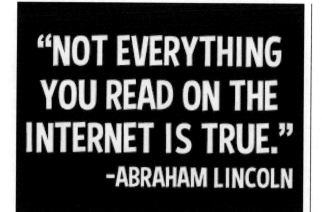

ONLINE TOOLS, TEMPLATES, AND WORKSHEETS

ASSIGNMENT:
Visit www.managementbuckets.com/20managementbuckets

☑ Click on a bucket.

☑ Download tools, templates, and worksheets.

EXAMPLES:

#1. The Results Bucket	**WORKSHEET #1.2:** "When the Horse Is Dead, Dismount." Download this PDF and check the Top-5 answers you often hear in your organization.
#16. The Delegation Bucket	**WORKSHEET #16.1:** "Dysfunctional Delegation Diseases." Take this Delegation Gut-Check Assessment and diagnose the severity of your delegation diseases. Are you a Code Green, Code Yellow, or Code Red?
#20. The Meetings Bucket	**WORKSHEET #20.1:** "Weekly Update to My Supervisor." Download this two-page Word document and ask each of your direct reports to customize it for your weekly one-on-one staff meetings. (Read Chapter 20. If this form was good enough for a Harvard Business School case study, maybe it's good enough for you!)

MANAGEMENT BUCKETS SELF-ASSESSMENT TOOL

Every CEO, senior leader and manager has unique strengths and competencies in many "management buckets"—but rarely does one person score high in all 20 buckets. *The Mastering the Management Buckets Self-Assessment Tool* helps leaders identify their strengths and weaknesses—and create a practical action plan to build the organization around their strengths, but not neglect areas outside their passion. Leaders (and their direct reports) must avoid the Head-in-Sand Syndrome and make a frank self-assessment of what level they're at in each of the 99 Knowledge Management Core Competencies of the 20 Management Buckets.

Moving from the "Head-in-Sand Syndrome" to the "Good to Great System"

Level 1	Red	I don't know what I don't know.
Level 2	Yellow	I know what I don't know.
Level 3	Green	I have an action plan to address what I know I don't know.
Level 4	Blue	I am knowledgeable and effective in this Core Competency.

THE MANAGEMENT BUCKETS SELF-ASSESSMENT TOOL Here are 20 of the 99 core competencies. ☑ Check where you're at today➔	LEVEL 1 RED	LEVEL 2 YELLOW	LEVEL 3 GREEN	LEVEL 4 BLUE
1. **THE BOARD BUCKET.** A nominee to the board of directors asks if you use the Carver Policy Governance model—and whether or not you have a Board Policies Manual.				
2. **THE BOOK BUCKET.** A direct report is an extreme micromanager. What book should she read this week and what training should you recommend to her?				
3. **THE BUDGET BUCKET.** A new board treasurer wants to change your financial reporting format. What are the best practices recommended by ECFA and other organizations?				
4. **THE CRISIS BUCKET.** Yikes! A key team member just had a severe moral failure. What should you do in the first 24 hours?				
5. **THE CULTURE BUCKET.** A candidate for a VP position wants to interview your management team to better understand your "culture" and "core values." Will they all say the same thing?				
6. **THE CUSTOMER BUCKET.** There is disagreement between your board and staff regarding your primary customer vs. your supporting customers. What are the five key questions every organization must answer?				
7. **THE DELEGATION BUCKET.** Your supervisor observes that you tend to be weak on delegation. Whether she is correct or not, outline what your next steps will be.				
8. **THE DONOR BUCKET.** Only half of your board members are generous givers to your organization. What are the best practices other CEOs employ to foster generous giving?				
9. **THE DRUCKER BUCKET.** Give a brief review of at least two books you've read by Peter Drucker, the father of modern management—and discuss one Druckerism that has helped you become a more effective executive.				
10. **THE *HOOPLA!* BUCKET.** A valued team member comments that the unrelenting pressure and deadlines have created a tense work environment. How do you fix this?				
11. **THE MEETINGS BUCKET.** Patrick Lencioni's book, *Death By Meeting*, suggests every team should have four kinds of meetings. What are they?				

THE MANAGEMENT BUCKETS SELF-ASSESSMENT TOOL Here are 20 of the 99 core competencies. ☑ Check where you're at today➔	LEVEL 1 RED	LEVEL 2 YELLOW	LEVEL 3 GREEN	LEVEL 4 BLUE
12. THE OPERATIONS BUCKET. A new team member has been chastised every day for five days for "not following procedure." What's wrong—and what are the likely solutions?				
13. THE PEOPLE BUCKET. According to researchers, there are four basic "social styles," yet most leaders operate as if there's only one "right one"—their own! What are the four and what implications do they have for donors, customers, board members, volunteers, staff, family, spouses, etc.?				
14. THE PRINTING BUCKET. Yikes! The newsletter was just mailed to 10,000 people and there is an embarrassing typo. The 800 number goes to a bar, not your company! What are your short-term and long-term solutions to this systemic problem?				
15. THE PROGRAM BUCKET. Peter Drucker said you must "slough off yesterday." Explain the law of diminishing returns and how it impacts your top five programs, products or services.				
16. THE RESULTS BUCKET. Every CEO, senior leader and virtually every staff member should have 3 to 10 written annual "Standards of Performance." Explain how this works in your organization. Extra credit: Discuss "S.M.A.R.T." goals.				
17. THE STRATEGY BUCKET. A well-liked CEO of another organization just got fired. They were growing, but apparently lacked a strategic plan. What are the key elements in the strategic planning process?				
18. THE SYSTEMS BUCKET. You're good at launching new programs, but weak on bringing them to the finish line. The discipline of project management requires what competencies?				
19. THE TEAM BUCKET. A best-selling book says there are 34 talents that can be leveraged into strengths. What are your Top-5 Strengths, according to this Gallup research?				
20. THE VOLUNTEER BUCKET. A trusted volunteer (and generous giver) complains to you that volunteers are "second class citizens" in your organization. What are some of the best practices today in 21st century volunteer management?				
ADD UP YOUR SCORE➔				

Moving from the "Head-in-Sand Syndrome" to the "Good to Great System"

Level 1	Red	I don't know what I don't know.
Level 2	Yellow	I know what I don't know.
Level 3	Green	I have an action plan to address what I know I don't know.
Level 4	Blue	I am knowledgeable and effective in this Core Competency.

YOUR SELF-ASSESSMENT:

➔ **Add up** your **RED** and **YELLOW** scores: _____. What are your next steps on each of these?
➔ **Who is** holding you accountable for your **GREEN** action plans? What are the target dates?
➔ **Are you** consistently training others with your **BLUE** core competencies?

DOWNLOAD THIS SELF-ASSESSMENT:

http://managementbuckets.com/Websites/managementbuckets/images/Management_Buckets_Self-Assessment_Tool.pdf

MASTER LIST OF JOHN PEARSON'S BOOK REVIEWS: 2007 - 2017

THE POWER OF MOMENTS:
Why Certain Experiences Have Extraordinary Impact
by Chip Heath and Dan Heath[84]

JOHN'S 2017 BOOK-OF-THE-YEAR!

From John's review of *The Power of Moments*[85]:

PARENTS AND GRANDPARENTS. The dinner table question from Spanx founder Sara Blakely's dad: "What did you guys fail at this week?" (p. 130)

HR TEAM. On creating extraordinary moments on a team member's first day on the job: "Imagine if you treated a first date like a new employee." (p. 18)

MARKETING STAFF. "One simple diagnostic to gauge whether you've transcended the ordinary is if people feel the need to pull out their cameras. If they take pictures, it must be a special occasion." (p. 63)

FUNDRAISERS AND OTHERS. On the topic of unheralded achievements in the chapter, "Thinking in Moments," the authors ask: "We celebrate employees' tenure with organizations, but what about their accomplishments? Isn't a salesman's 10 millionth dollar of revenue earned worth commemorating? Or what about a talented manager who has had 10 direct reports promoted?" (p. 36)

And I'd add: And what about celebrating a single mom's faithful $10-a-month donor gifts when her total giving reaches the $500 or $1,000 milestone? That's a moment to celebrate! Plus, don't miss the creative way one organization sends personalized thank you notes to donors. (p. 151)

BOARD MEMBERS. Recently, I played the book's audio of "Clinic 1: The Missed Moments of Retail Banking" to my fellow board members at Christian Community Credit Union. The question, "Could banks learn to 'think in moments'?" Convicting—but very, very applicable to all organizations.

I could go on—but you get my drift. *This book changed—changed!—my thinking in so many ways.*

---

[84] Chip Heath and Dan Heath, *The Power of Moments: Why Certain Experiences Have Extraordinary Impact* (New York: Simon & Schuster, 2017)
[85] John Pearson, *Your Weekly Staff Meeting eNews* (Nov. 25, 2017): *http://urgentink.typepad.com/my_weblog/2017/11/the-power-of-moments.html*

DINOSAURS DIDN'T READ.

NOW THEY ARE EXTINCT.

Master List of John Pearson's Book Reviews
2007 – 2017*
Management, Leadership, and Governance
*through December 31, 2017

❑ **BOOK REVIEW ARCHIVES.** Almost 400 book reviews that have been featured in John Pearson's eNews, Your Weekly Staff Meeting are available in the Book Review Archives at: ➔www.urgentink.typepad.com

❑ **SUBSCRIBE.** Sign up for your complimentary subscription at:
➔www.managementbuckets.com/enews

❑ **DOWNLOAD.** Download three book lists at:
➔www.managementbuckets.com/book-bucket

3 Book Lists are posted:
☑ List #1: Books by Management Buckets Category
❑ List #2: Books by eNews Issue Number
❑ List #3: John Top-100 Book List (updated 12/31/16)

❑ **SEARCH FOR A BOOK REVIEW.** To find a book (from this master list on the following pages:
➔Google "[the book title], John Pearson's Buckets Blog"

CFO asks CEO: "What happens if we invest in developing our people and then they leave us?" CEO: "What happens if we don't and they stay?"	**Leaders Are Readers (and Listeners!): Delegate Your Reading!**
	❑ Each month, give your direct reports one book to read.
	❑ Ask for a 5- to 10-minute "book review" from one person each week.
	❑ Your team will be inspired, motivated and their learning will be enriched from reading…
	…4 books x 11 months = 44 books per year!
	❑ Then…file the book on your staff resource shelf with your marked-up copies so your managers can mentor their people with niche chapters.

For more ideas on creating a lifelong learning culture, read the Book Bucket chapter in
Mastering the Management Buckets
and visit
➔www.managementbuckets.com/book-bucket

BOOK-OF-THE-YEAR HONORS

John Pearson has been selecting the "Book-of-the-Year" honors since 2008:

2017 Book-of-the-Year
❑ 372. *The Power of Moments: Why Certain Experiences Have Extraordinary Impact,* by Chip Heath and Dan Heath

The Big Idea:
Defy "the forgettable flatness of everyday work and life by creating a few precious moments."

Read John's review:
http://urgentink.typepad.com/my_weblog/2017/11/the-power-of-moments.html

2016 Book-of-the-Year
❑ 342. *The ONE Thing: The Surprisingly Simple Truth Behind Extraordinary Results,* by Gary Keller with Jay Papasan

"What's the ONE Thing
you can do this week such that by doing it
everything else would be easier or unnecessary?"

Read John's review:
http://urgentink.typepad.com/my_weblog/2016/05/the-one-thing.html

2016 Runner-up
❑ 345. *Team of Teams: New Rules of Engagement for a Complex World* by Gen. Stanley McChrystal with Tantum Collins, David Silverman, and Chris Fussell.

2016 Runner-up
❑ 344. *The Ideal Team Player: How to Recognize and Cultivate the Three Essential Virtues* by Patrick Lencioni

Read John's reviews:

☑ *Team of Teams* - http://urgentink.typepad.com/my_weblog/2016/06/team-of-teams.html

☑ *The Ideal Team Player* - http://urgentink.typepad.com/my_weblog/2016/06/the-ideal-team-player.html

BOOK-OF-THE-YEAR HONORS
http://urgentink.typepad.com/my_weblog/2017/04/book-of-the-year-honors-2008-to-2016.html

John Pearson has been selecting the "Book-of-the-Year" honors since 2008:

2008

☐ 87. *The Five Most Important Questions You Will Ever Ask About Your Organization*, by Peter Drucker (plus Collins, Kotler, Kouzes, Rodin, Rangan and Hesselbein)

2009

☐ 168 & 181. *Strengthening the Soul of Your Leadership: Seeking God in the Crucible of Ministry*, by Ruth Haley Barton

2010

☐ 191 & 328. *The First 90 Days: Proven Strategies for Getting Up to Speed Faster and Smarter* (Updated and Expanded), by Michael Watkins

2011

☐ 208. *Necessary Endings: The Employees, Businesses, and Relationships That All of Us Have to Give Up in Order to Move Forward,* by Dr. Henry Cloud

2012

☐ 245. *The Advantage: Why Organizational Health Trumps Everything Else in Business*, by Patrick Lencioni

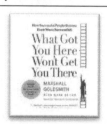

2013

☐ 269. *What Got You Here Won't Get You There: Discover the 20 Workplace Habits You Need to Break,* by Marshall Goldsmith and Mark Reiter

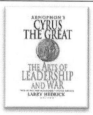

2014

☐ 301. *Xenophon's Cyrus the Great: The Arts of Leadership and War*, by Xenophon (Larry Hedrick, Editor)

2015

☐ 318. *Leadership Briefs: Shaping Organizational Culture to Stretch Leadership Capacity* by Dick Daniels

Read insights from all 20 buckets every year!
MASTERING THE MANAGEMENT BUCKETS
20 CRITICAL COMPETENCIES FOR LEADING
YOUR BUSINESS OR NONPROFIT

http://managementbuckets.com/20managementbuckets

Cause ◆ Community ◆ Corporation
The 20 Management Buckets are organized into three arenas—think three-legged stool. So when you read (or clip or download an article), categorize the resource into one of these 20 buckets. See the book or the website for the core competency statement/description for each bucket.

OUR CAUSE
#1: The Results Bucket
#2: The Customer Bucket
#3: The Strategy Bucket
#4: The Drucker Bucket
#5: The Book Bucket
#6: The Program Bucket

OUR COMMUNITY
#7: The People Bucket
#8: The Culture Bucket
#9: The Team Bucket
#10: The *Hoopla!* Bucket
#11: The Donor Bucket
#12: The Volunteer Bucket
#13: The Crisis Bucket

OUR CORPORATION
#14: The Board Bucket
#15: The Budget Bucket
#16: The Delegation Bucket
#17: The Operations Bucket
#18: The Systems Bucket
#19: The Printing Bucket
#20: The Meetings Bucket

http://amzn.to/2Cw0LcS

THE CAUSE
To read a book review (and order the book), click on "Archives" at
www.urgentink.typepad.com
or Google "[the book title], John Pearson's Buckets Blog"

Top-10 Book = Named one of the "Top-10 Books" reviewed in that year by John Pearson (effective 2008).
▶Book-of-the-Year = Named "Book-of-the-Year" by John Pearson (effective 2008).
The 2018 honors will be announced December 31, 2018 in *Your Weekly Staff Meeting* eNews.

#1. The Results Bucket (By Issue Number and Book Review Date)

❏ 23. Stop Setting Goals If You Would Rather Solve Problems
Biehl, Bobb (2/5/2007)

❏ 29. Execution: The Discipline of Getting Things Done
Bossidy, Larry and Charan, Ram (3/19/2007)

❏ 44. Leaving Microsoft to Change the World: An Entrepreneur's Odyssey to Educate the World's Children
Wood, John (7/9/2007)

❏ 51. The Three Signs of a Miserable Job: A Fable for Managers
Lencioni, Patrick (8/27/2007)

❏ 53. Effectiveness by the Number: Counting What Counts in Church
Hoyt, William R. (9/10/2007)

❏ 57. Confronting Reality: Doing What Matters to Get Things Right
Bossidy, Larry and Charan, Ram (10/8/2007)

❏ 68. Reveal: Where Are You?
Hawkins, Greg and Parkinson, Cally (12/24/2007)

❏ 70. Mastering the Management Buckets: 20 Critical Competencies for Leading Your Business or Nonprofit - Pearson, John (1/8/2008)

❏ 72. *The Five Temptations of a CEO
Lencioni, Patrick (1/21/2008) Top-10 Book

❏ 92. & 93. Know Can Do! Put Your Know-How Into Action
Blanchard, Ken; Meyer, Paul J.; Ruhe, Dick (6/9/2008)

❏ 97. Managing the Nonprofit Organization: Principles and Practices
Drucker, Peter F. (7/21/2008)

❏ 107. Squawk! How to Stop Making Noise and Start Getting Results
Bradberry, Travis (9/29/2008)

❏ 118. The 80/20 Principle: The Secret to Achieving More With Less
Koch, Richard (12/15/2008)

❏ 149. *How the Mighty Fall: And Why Some Companies Never Give In
Collins, Jim (7/28/2009) Top-10 Book

❏ 158. *Master Leaders: Revealing Conversations With 30 Leadership Greats
Barna, George with Dallas, Bill (10/5/2009) Top-10 Book

❏ 164. Missional Renaissance: Changing the Scorecard for the Church
McNeal, Reggie (11/20/2009)

❏ 167. The Most Effective Organization in the U.S.: Leadership Secrets of The Salvation Army
Watson, Robert A. and Brown, Ben (12/14/2009)

❏ 174. Churchill
Johnson, Paul (2/22/2010)

❏ 190. The Nonprofit Dashboard: A Tool for Tracking Progress
Butler, Lawrence M. (7/17/2010)

❏ 199. Leading Without Power: Finding Hope in Serving Community
De Pree, Max (10/18/2010)

▶2011 Book-of-the-Year
❏ 208. *Necessary Endings: The Employees, Businesses, and Relationships That All of Us Have to Give Up in Order to Move Forward - Cloud, Dr. Henry (2/7/2011)

❏ 232. I Want to Make a Difference Now: Your Bridge to Global Impact
Parrott, Don (10/3/2011)

❏ 242. Tales from the Top: 10 Crucial Questions from the World's #1 Executive Coach
Alexander, Graham (1/31/2012)

❏ 255. Corporate Entrepreneurship: How to Create a Thriving Entrepreneurial Spirit Throughout Your Company - Hisrich, Robert D. and Kearney, Claudine (8/13/2012)

❏ 279. Entrepreneurial Leadership: Finding Your Calling, Making a Difference
Goossen, Richard J. and Stevens, R. Paul (6/9/2013) Top-10 Book

❏ 297. The Choice: The Christ-Centered Pursuit of Kingdom Outcomes
by Gary G. Hoag, R. Scott Rodin, and Wesley K. Willmer (4/13/2014) Top-10 Book

▶2015 Book-of-the-Year
❏ 318. Leadership Briefs: Shaping Organizational Culture to Stretch Leadership Capacity, by Dick Daniels (2/21/15)

▶2016 Book-of-the-Year
❏ 342. The ONE Thing: The Surprisingly Simple Truth Behind Extraordinary Results
by Gary Keller with Jay Papasan (5/2/16)

❏ 361, 362. The Gatekeepers: How the White House Chiefs of Staff Define Every Presidency
Chris Whipple (6/13/17, 6/21/17) `Top-10 Book`

> **RICHARD STEARNS:**
>
> "Leaders have to be very aware of the power they wield. When you're at the bottom of the hierarchical ladder, sometimes you have to shout to be heard, because you don't have any title or you don't have authority. But when you are the CEO or a top leader, you can speak softly and it sounds like a shout to someone. So when you criticize someone, you have to be very careful about being too blunt or cutting, because whatever you say will be amplified ten times just because you're the president. You have to adapt your style to realize that it's not just you, the person, speaking; it's the position that you hold that's speaking."

#2. The Customer Bucket (By Issue Number and Book Review Date)

❏ 6. Applebee's America: How Successful Political, Business and Religious Leaders Connect With the New American Community - Sosnik, Douglas B., Dowd, Matthew J., and Fournier, Ron (10/2/2006)

❏ 8. Versatile Selling: Adapting Your Style So Customers Say "Yes!"
Wilson Learning (10/16/2006)

❏ 19. Citizen Brand: 10 Commandments for Transforming Brands in a Consumer Democracy
Gobe, Marc (1/8/2007)

❏ 24. Sales Autopsy: 50 Postmortems Reveal What Killed the Sale (and What Might Have Saved It
Seidman, Dan (2/12/2007)

❏ 49. The Marketing Mavens
Capon, Noel (8/13/2007)

❏ 99. *Duct Tape Marketing: The World's Most Practical Small Business Marketing Guide
Jantsch, John (8/4/2008) `Top-10 Book`

❏ 116. *Outliers: The Story of Success
Gladwell, Malcolm (12/1/2008) `Top-10 Book`

❏ 127. Tribes: We Need You to Lead Us
Godin, Seth (2/16/2009)

❏ 133. *The King of Madison Avenue: David Ogilvy and the Making of Modern Advertising
Roman, Kenneth (3/31/2009) `Top-10 Book`

❏ 144. *Wired to Care: How Companies Prosper When They Create Widespread Empathy
Patnaik, Dev with Mortensen, Peter (6/16/2009) `Top-10 Book`

❏ 148. The Church & the Parachurch: An Uneasy Marriage
White, Jerry (7/21/2009)

❐ 175. *Getting Naked: A Business Fable About Shedding the Three Fears That Sabotage Client Loyalty
Lencioni, Patrick (3/3/2010) `Top-10 Book`

❐ 183. Muslims, Christians, and Jesus: Understanding and Building Relationships
Medearis, Carl (5/6/2010)

❐ 184. Managing the Millennials: Discover the Core Competencies for Managing Today's Workforce
Espinoza, Chip; Ukleja, Mick and Rusch, Craig (5/14/2010)

❐ 210. It's the Customer, Stupid! 34 Wake-up Calls to Help You Stay Client-Focused
Aun, Michael A. (3/4/2011)

❐ 247. The Mindset List of American History: From Typewriters to Text Messages—What Ten Generations of Americans Think Is Normal - McBride, Tom and Nief, Ron (4/16/2012)

❐ 282. *Outliers: The Story of Success
Gladwell, Malcolm (7/31/2013) `Top-10 Book` - *Summer Classic Book Series*, repeated from Issue 116

❐ 305. Muslims, Christians, and Jesus: Understanding and Building Relationships
by Carl Medearis (8/15/14)

❐ 323. TRUST: The Firm Foundation of Kingdom Fruitfulness,
by Dan Busby (4/14/15) `Top-10 Book`

❐ 330B. Gospel Justice: Joining Together to Provide Help & Hope for Those Oppressed by Legal Injustice,
by Bruce Strom (8/26/15)

❐ 340A REBRAND: Workbook + Coloring Sheets for Ministry Branding
by Jason Pearson (3/21/16) `Top-10 Book`

#3. The Strategy Bucket (By Issue Number and Book Review Date)

❐ 1. Good to Great and the Social Sectors
Collins, Jim (8/28/2006)

❐ 47. What Were They Thinking? Unconventional Wisdom About Management
Pfeffer, Jeffrey (7/30/2007)

❐ 85. Simply Strategic Stuff: Help for Leaders Drowning in the Details of Running a Church
Stevens, Tim & Morgan, Tony (4/21/2008)

❐ 94. The Prince
Machiavelli, Niccolo (translated by Peter Constantine) (6/30/2008)

❐ 100. *Six Disciplines® Execution Revolution: Solving the One Business Problem That Makes Solving All Other Problems Easier - Harpst, Gary (8/11/2008) `Top-10 Book`

❐ 140. 101 Mission Statements From Top Companies: Plus Guidelines for Writing Your Own Mission Statement - Abrahams, Jeffrey (5/19/2009)

❏ 147. Being Indian: The Truth About Why the 21st Century Will Be India's
Varma, Pavan K. (7/16/2009)

❏ 151. Harvard Business Review on Managing Through a Downturn (collection of 7 articles)
Harvard Business Review (8/12/2009)

❏ 159. Well Connected: Releasing Power, Restoring Hope Through Kingdom Partnerships
Butler, Phill (10/14/2009)

❏ 160. The Longview: Lasting Strategies for Rising Leaders
Parrott, Roger (10/23/2009)

❏ 179. Driving Strategic Planning: A Nonprofit Executive's Guide (Second Edition)
Waechter, Susan A. (4/1/2010)

❏ 182. Visioneering: God's Blueprint for Developing and Maintaining Personal Vision
Stanley, Andy (4/26/2010)

❏ 185. In the Shadow of the Moon (DVD – documentary)
Sington, David (Director) (5/24/2010)

❏ 188. Good to Great: Why Some Companies Make the Leap…and Others Don't
Collins, Jim (6/28/2010)

❏ 217. *Little Bets: How Breakthrough Ideas Emerge From Small Discoveries
Sims, Peter (5/13/2011) Top-10 Book

❏ 225. Jesus Calling: Enjoying Peace in His Presence
Young, Sarah (8/4/2011)

❏ 235. *Great by Choice: Uncertainty, Chaos, and Luck—Why Some Thrive Despite Them All
Collins, Jim and Hansen, Morten T. (11/8/2011) Top-10 Book

❏ 251. Beyond Performance Management: Why, When and How to Use 40 Tools and Best Practices for Superior Business Performance - Hope, Jeremy and Player, Steve (6/12/2012)

❏ 257. *Nonprofit Financial Sustainability: Making Strategic Decisions for Financial Viability
Bell, Jeanne; Masaoka, Jan and Zimmerman, Steve (9/30/2012) Top-10 Book

❏ 261. *Thinkpak: A Brainstorming Card Deck
Michalko, Michael (11/26/2012) Top-10 Book

❏ 270. The Pope & The CEO: John Paul II's Leadership Lessons to a Young Swiss Guard
Widner, Andreas (2/28/2013)

❏ 278. Rumsfeld's Rules: Leadership Lessons in Business, Politics, War, and Life
Rumsfeld, Donald (5/31/2013) Top-10 Book

❏ 280. HBR's 10 Must Reads on Strategy (including the featured article "What Is Strategy?")
Porter, Michael E. (6/23/2013)

❏ 289. David and Goliath: Underdogs, Misfits, and the Art of Battling Giants
Gladwell, Malcolm (12/4/2013) `Top-10 Book`

❏ 303A. Nonprofit Kit for Dummies® (4th Edition)
by Stan Hutton and Frances N. Phillips (includes a CD-ROM with 100+ documents) – (7/12/2014)

❏ 307. The Leader's SEEcret: Asking the Right Questions and Embracing God's Answers
by Skip Garmo (9/13/2014)

❏ 319. Breakthrough: Unleashing the Power of a Proven Plan,
by Randon A. Samelson (3/13/15) `Top-10 Book`

❏ 330C. Better Together: Discovering the Dynamic Results of Cooperation, by Paul Fleischmann (8/26/15)

❏ 332. The Attacker's Advantage: Turning Uncertainty Into Breakthrough Opportunities,
by Ram Charan (11/5/15) `Top-10 Book`

❏ 334A. Playing to Win: How Strategy Really Works,
by A.G. Lafley and Roger L. Martin (12/3/15)

❏ 334B. The Big Lie of Strategic Planning,
by Roger L. Martin (Harvard Business Review) – (12/3/15)

❏ 337A. 5: Where Will You Be Five Years from Today?
by Dan Zadra (1/20/16)

❏ 345. Team of Teams: New Rules of Engagement for a Complex World
by Gen. Stanley McChrystal with Tantum Collins, David Silverman, and Chris Fussell (6/28/16) `Top-10 Book`

❏ 357. Managing Transitions: Making the Most of Change (25th Anniversary Edition),
by William Bridges (4/5/17) `Top-10 Book`

❏ 359. Barna Trends 2017: What's New and What's Next at the Intersection of Faith and Culture, by Barna
(Roxanne Stone, Editor-in-Chief) (5/12/17) `Top-10 Book`

❏ 365. Leading the Other Way: How to Change the Church Planting World
JD Pearring (8/8/17)

❏ 368, 369A, 370. Illuminate: Ignite Change Through Speeches, Stories, Ceremonies, and Symbols, by
Nancy Duarte and Patti Sanchez (9/13/17, 9/27/17, 10/11/17) `Top-10 Book`

The Contrarian's Guide to Leadership,
by Steven Sample (former president of USC):

From John Pearson's review:

"Addicted to newspapers, he once went six months without reading one—but stayed current through the art of listening. This chapter is worth the price of the book. It's contrarian and refreshing. It changed my thinking. How often does a book do that for you?"

#4. The Drucker Bucket (By Issue Number and Book Review Date)

❏ 20. The Effective Executive: The Definitive Guide to Getting the Right Things Done
Drucker, Peter (1/15/2007)

❏ 31. The Temptation to Do Good
Drucker, Peter (4/2/2007)

❏ 61. Breakfast With Fred
Smith, Sr., Fred (11/5/2007)

▶**2008 Book-of-the-Year**
❏ 87. *The Five Most Important Questions You Will Ever Ask About Your Organization
Drucker, Peter (plus Collins, Kotler, Kouzes, Rodin, Rangan and Hesselbein) - (5/5/2008)

❏ 154. Myself and Other More Important Matters
Handy, Charles (9/2/2009)

❏ 178. The Daily Drucker: 366 Days of Insight and Motivation for Getting the Right Things Done
Drucker, Peter F. and Maciariello, Joseph A. (3/25/2010)

❏ 215. Leadership Smarts: Inspiration and Wisdom from the Heart of a Leader
Blanchard, Ken (4/21/2011)

❏ 243. A Class With Drucker: The Lost Lessons of the World's Greatest Management Teacher
Cohen, William (2/10/2012)

❏ 281. The Temptation to Do Good
Drucker, Peter (7/7/2013) – *Summer Classic Book Series*, repeated from Issue 31

❏ 283. Wisdom from Lyle E. Schaller: The Elder Statesman of Church Leadership
Bird, Warren (8/4/2013)

❏ 288. Bring TIM: Time Is Money—the Meeting Cost Calculator
Manufactured by Bring Tim LLC (11/9/2013)

❏ 292. The Practical Drucker: Applying the Wisdom of the World's Greatest Management Thinker
by William A. Cohen (1/15/2014)

❏ 298. Drucker & Me: What a Texas Entrepreneur Learned from the Father of Modern Management
by Bob Buford (4/24/14) Top-10 Book

▶**2014 Book-of-the-Year**
❏ 301. Xenophon's Cyrus the Great: The Arts of Leadership and War
by Xenophon (Larry Hedrick, Editor) – (6/11/14)

❑ 316. A Year With Peter Drucker: 52 Weeks of Coaching for Leadership Effectiveness, by Joseph A. Maciariello (1/6/15) `Top-10 Book`

- Note: Visit the blog posts of 52 guest writers for their color commentaries on all 52 chapters at http://www.urgentink.typepad.com/drucker_mondays/

❑ 331A. *Peter Drucker's Five Most Important Questions: Enduring Wisdom for Today's Leaders, by Peter F. Drucker, Frances Hesselbein, and Joan Snyder Kuhl (10/14/15) `Top-10 Book`

❑ 346. The Presidents Club: Inside the World's Most Exclusive Fraternity (Summer Rerun from Issue 252) by Nancy Gibbs and Michael Duff (7/12/16)

#5. The Book Bucket (By Issue Number and Book Review Date) – "The Catch-all Bucket"

❑ 3. You Can't Win a Fight With Your Boss & 55 Other Rules For Success
Markert, Tom (9/11/2006)

❑ 5. A Diary of Private Prayer
Baillie, John (9/25/2006)

❑ 13. TrueFaced: Trust God and Others With Who You Really Are
Thrall, Bill; McNicol, Bruce and Lynch, John (11/20/2006)

❑ 16. Taking the Lead: Following the Example of Paul, Timothy and Silvanus
Jenson, Ron (12/11/2006)

❑ 17. Fit After 40: 3 Keys to Looking Good & Feeling Great
Nava, Don (12/18/2006)

❑ 18. The Life You've Always Wanted: Spiritual Disciplines for Ordinary People
Ortberg, John (1/2/2007)

❑ 22. The Best Question Ever: A Revolutionary Approach to Decision-making
Stanley, Andy (1/29/2007)

❑ 25. Balancing Life's Demands: A New Perspective on Priorities
Howard, J. Grant (2/19/2007)

❑ 30. Winning: The Answers--Confronting 74 of the Toughest Questions in Business Today
Welch, Jack and Suzy (3/26/2007)

❑ 41. Tales from Q School: Inside Golf's Fifth Major
Feinstein, John (6/11/2007)

❑ 42. A Long Obedience in the Same Direction
Peterson, Eugene H. (6/18/2007)

❑ 45. Zing! Five Steps and 101 Tips for Creativity on Command
Harrison, Sam (7/16/2007)

❑ 56. Gilead
Robinson, Marilynne (10/1/2007)

❏ 63. The Mulligan: Everyone Needs a Second Chance in Golf and in Life
Armstrong, Wally and Blanchard, Ken (11/19/2007)

❏ 76. Experiencing God: Knowing and Doing the Will of God
Blackaby, Henry T. and King, Claude V. (2/18/2008)

❏ 79. Brain Rules: 12 Principles for Surviving and Thriving at Work, Home and School
Median, John (3/10/2008)

❏ 80. Devotional Classics: Selected Readings for Individuals and Groups (2005 Revised Edition)
Foster, Richard J. and Smith, James Bryan   (3/17/2008)

❏ 81. The Contrarian's Guide to Leadership
Sample, Steven (3/24/2008)

❏ 90. *Same Kind of Different As Me: A Modern-Day Slave, an International Art Dealer, and the Unlikely
Woman Who Bound Them Together - Hall, Ron and Moore, Denver (5/27/2008) `Top-10 Book`

❏ 95. Put Down the Duckie (DVD)
Sesame Street (7/8/2008)

❏ 108. The Essential Bible Guide: 100 Readings Through the World's Most Important Book
Kuniholm, Whitney (10/8/2008)

❏ 112. Operation World: When We Pray God Works (21st Century Edition)
Johnstone, Patrick (11/4/2008)

❏ 121. The Message/Remix: Solo: An Uncommon Devotional
Peterson, Eugene H. (1/6/2009)

❏ 136. The CIA World Factbook 2009
CIA (4/22/2009)

❏ 139. *The Prodigal God: Recovering the Heart of the Christian Faith
Keller, Timothy (5/12/2009) `Top-10 Book`

❏ 142. *The 100 Best Business Books of All Time: What They Say, Why They Matter, and How They Can
Help You - Covert, Jack and Sattersten, Todd (6/2/2009) `Top-10 Book`

❏ 143. What Are You Living For? Investing Your Life in What Matters Most
Williams, Pat (6/10/2009)

❏ 150. Life Among the Lutherans
Keillor, Garrison (8/4/2009)

❏ 165. What Difference Do It Make? Stories of Hope and Healing
Hall, Ron and Moore, Denver (and Vincent, Lynn) (11/25/2009)

❏ 193. Leadership Prayers
Kriegbaum, Richard (8/13/2010)

❏ 213. *Chasing Francis
Cron, Ian Morgan (4/6/2011) `Top-10 Book`

❏ 219. Rules to Live By: 52 Principles for a Better Life
White, Jerry (6/14/2011)
❏ 220. The Ambition
Strobel, Lee (6/22/2011)

❏ 224. Besides the Bible: 100 Books That Have, Should or Will Create Christian Culture
Gibson, Dan; Green, Jordan and Pattison, John (7/25/2011)

❏ 237. Invisible Neighbors: If You Don't See Them, You're Not Looking
Ashmen, John (12/13/2011)

❏ 246. Crafting a Rule of Life: An Invitation to a Well-Ordered Way
Macchia, Stephen A. (4/6/2012)

❏ 268. A Stroke of Grace
Zander, Dieter and Witmer, LaDonna (1/31/2013)

❏ 275. My Ideal Bookshelf
Mount, Jane (art) and La Force, Thessaly (editor) (4/19/2013)

❏ 277. Spiritual Discernment Retreat Guide
Macchia, Stephen A. (5/23/2013)

❏ 286. On My Worst Day: Cheesecake, Evil, Sandy Koufax and Jesus
Lynch, John (10/8/2013) `Top-10 Book`

❏ 290. The Messiah: An Oratorio for Four-Part Chorus of Mixed Voices, Soprano, Alto, Tenor and Bass
Soli and Piano, by Handel, G.F. (12/23/13) - **Merry Christmas!**

❏ 299. Leadership Prayers
by Richard Kriegbaum (5/20/14)

❏ 310A. Monday Morning Atheist: Why You Switch God Off at Work
by Doug Spada and Dave Scott (10/27/2014)

❏ 310B. The Switch: Your Monday Revolution (Six Weeks to God's Power on Monday) – Book + Guide + DVD – by Doug Spada (10/27/2014)

❏ 312. Let Your Life Speak: Listening for the Voice of Vocation
by Parker J. Palmer (11/22/14) `Top-10 Book`

❏ 314. Wellspring: 31 Days to Whole-Hearted Living
by Stephen Macchia (12/22/14)

❏ 326. Soul Keeping: Caring for the Most Important Part of You,
by John Ortberg (6/10/15) `Top-10 Book`

❏ 341. Serve Strong: Biblical Encouragement to Sustain God's Servants
By Terry Powell (4/13/16)

❏ 350. The Time of Our Lives
by Peggy Noonan (9/11/16) `Top-10 Book`

❏ 353B. Steward Leader Meditations: Fifty Devotions for the Leadership Journey
by R. Scott Rodin (12/23/16)

❏ 357B. **Book-of-the-Year Honors: 2008 to 2016** (4/21/17)
Note: This special blog was not sent via email but is posted online only at:
http://urgentink.typepad.com/my_weblog/2017/04/book-of-the-year-honors-2008-to-2016.html

#6. The Program Bucket (By Issue Number and Book Review Date)

❏ 52. Marketing Your Ministry: 10 Critical Principles

John Pearson and Robert Hisrich (9/3/2007)

Order: http://amzn.to/2CxLvKZ

❏ 172. PastorPreneur: Pastors and Entrepreneurs Answer the Call
Jackson, John (1/28/2010)

❏ 189. Creators: From Chaucer and Durer to Picasso and Disney
Johnson, Paul (7/6/2010)

❏ 205. Entrepreneurship
Hisrich, Robert D.; Peters, Michael P. and Shepherd, Dean A. (12/23/2010)

❏ 351. Outrageous: Awake to the Unexpected Adventures of Everyday Faith
by Aaron Tredway (10/27/16) `Top-10 Book`

THE COMMUNITY
To read a book review (and order the book), click on "Archives" at
www.urgentink.typepad.com
or Google "[the book title], John Pearson's Buckets Blog"

Top-10 Book = Named one of the "Top-10 Books" reviewed in that year by John Pearson (effective 2008).
▶Book-of-the-Year = Named "Book-of-the-Year" by John Pearson (effective 2008).
The 2018 honors will be announced December 31, 2018 in *Your Weekly Staff Meeting* eNews.

#7. The People Bucket (By Issue Number and Book Review Date)

❏ 67. How to Deal With Annoying People: What to Do When You Can't Avoid Them
Phillips, Bob and Alyn, Kimberly (12/17/2007)

❏ 71. Life's a Campaign: What Politics Has Taught Me About Friendship, Rivalry, Reputation and Success
Matthews, Chris (1/14/2008)

❏ 105. The Great Connection--A Story That Reveals Life's Most Important Lesson: How to Connect With
Others—Especially Yourself - Warren, Arnie (9/16/2008)

❏ 115. The Social Styles Handbook: Find Your Comfort Zone and Make People Feel Comfortable With You
Wilson Learning Library (11/24/2008)

❏ 201. Managing Your Boss (*Harvard Business Review* article)
Gabarro, John J. and Kotter, John P. (11/8/2010)

❏ 262. *7 Seconds to Success: How to Effectively Relate to People in an Instant
Coffey, Gary and Phillips, Bob (12/8/2012) Top-10 Book

❏ 271. We Have a Pope (Habemus Papam) - (DVD, English subtitles)
Moretti, Nanni (Director) - (3/11/2013)

❏ 300. Jesus: A Biography from a Believer
by Paul Johnson (5/29/2014)

❏ 343. Social Style: The Ah Ha's of Effective Relationships
by Gerald L. Prince and John R. Myers (5/2616)

❏ 366. Top Ten Ways to Be a Great Leader
Hans Finzel (8/18/17)

#8. The Culture Bucket (By Issue Number and Book Review Date)

❏ 37. The Peacemaker: A Biblical Guide to Resolving Personal Conflict
Sande, Ken (5/14/2007)

❏ 74. Heroic Leadership: Best Practices From a 450-Year-Old Company That Changed the World
Lowney, Chris (2/4/2008)

❏ 75. Coach Wooden One-on-One: Inspiring Conversations on Purpose, Passion and the Pursuit of Success - Wooden, John and Carty, Jay (2/11/2008)

❏ 126. The Character of Leadership: Nine Qualities That Define Great Leaders
Iorg, Jeff (2/9/2009)

❏ 132. Lessons From San Quentin: Everything I Need to Know About Life I Learned in Prison
Dallas, Bill with Barna, George (3/23/2009)

❏ 135. The Short List: In a Life Full of Choices, There Are Only Four That Matter
Butterworth, Bill (4/13/2009)

❏ 141. Humility
Murray, Andrew (5/26/2009)

❏ 177. Leading Across Cultures: Effective Ministry and Mission in the Global Church
Plueddemann, James E. (3/20/2010)

❏ 186. *The Speed of Trust: The One Thing That Changes Everything
Covey, Stephen M.R. (6/7/2010) `Top-10 Book`

❏ 187. *Delivering Happiness: A Path to Profits, Passion, and Purpose
Hsieh, Tony (6/16/2010) `Top-10 Book`

❏ 192. Kiss, Bow or Shake Hands: The Bestselling Guide to Doing Business in More than 60 Countries
Morrison, Terri and Conaway, Wayne A. (7/30/2010)

196. *The Steward Leader: Transforming People, Organizations and Communities
Rodin, R. Scott (9/16/2010) `Top-10 Book`

❏ 203. The Inner Ring
Lewis, C.S. (12/3/2010)

❏ 229. *The Company Culture Challenge
Betzel, Robert and Russell, David (9/2/2011) `Top-10 Book`

▶2012 Book-of-the-Year
❏ 245. *The Advantage: Why Organizational Health Trumps Everything Else in Business
Lencioni, Patrick (3/23/2012)

❏ 254. *Pursuing God's Will Together: A Discernment Practice for Leadership Groups
Barton, Ruth Haley (7/24/2012) `Top-10 Book`

❏ 258. Make Your Values Mean Something (*Harvard Business Review* article)
Lencioni, Patrick (10/9/2012)

▶**2013 Book-of-the-Year**
❏ 269. What Got You Here Won't Get You There: Discover the 20 Workplace Habits You Need to Break
Goldsmith, Marshall and Reiter, Mark (2/18/2013)

❏ 274. The Leader's Palette: Seven Primary Colors
Enlow, Jr., Ralph E. (4/12/2013) `Top-10 Book`

❏ 302. The Student Leadership Challenge: Five Practices for Becoming an Exemplary Leader
by James M. Kouzes and Barry Z. Posner (6/30/2014)

❏ 303B. Leadership for Dummies®
by Marshall Loeb and Stephen Kindel (7/12/2014)

❏ 304. Tales from the Top: 10 Crucial Questions from the World's #1 Executive Coach
by Graham Alexander (8/11/14)

❏ 324. The Power of Passion in Leadership: Lead From Your Heart, Not Just Your Head,
by Hans Finzel (4/21/15)

❏ 330A. Invisible Neighbors: If You Don't See Them, You're Not Looking, by John Ashmen (8/26/15 – revised)

❏ 333. Little Victories: Perfect Rules for Imperfect Living, by Jason Gay (11/25/15)

❏ 335. Broken and Whole: A Leader's Path to Spiritual Transformation,
by Stephen Macchia (12/24/15) `Top-10 Book`

#9. The Team Bucket (By Issue Number and Book Review Date)

❏ 2. A Tale of Three Kings: A Study in Brokenness
Edwards, Gene (9/4/2006)

❏ 4. Now, Discover Your Strengths
Buckingham, Marcus & Clifton, Donald (9/18/2006)

❏ 15. Becoming a Healthy Team: 5 Traits of Vital Leadership
Macchia, Stephen A. (12/4/2006)

❏ 33. For Your Improvement: A Guide for Development and Coaching
Lombardo, Michael M. and Eichinger, Robert W. (4/16/2007)

❏ 46. StrengthsFinder 2.0
Rath, Tom (7/23/2007)

❏ 48. Cure for the Common Life: Living in Your Sweet Spot
Lucado, Max (8/6/2007)

❏ 54. Twelve O'clock High (DVD, 1949)
King, Henry (Director) - (9/18/2007)

❏ 55. Ten Thousand Horses: How Leaders Harness Raw Potential for Extraordinary Results
Stahl-Wert, John and Jennings, Ken (9/24/2007)

❏ 62. Choosing to Cheat: Who Wins When Family and Work Collide
Stanley, Andy (11/12/2007)

❏ 65. Leadership Is an Art
De Pree, Max (12/4/2007)

❏ 66. Building Successful Teams
Butterworth, Bill (12/10/2007)

❏ 73. Leaders at All Levels: Deepening Your Talent Pool to Solve the Succession Crisis
Charan, Ram (1/28/2008)

❏ 77. Fired Up or Burned Out: How to Reignite Your Team's Passion, Creativity and Productivity
Stallard, Michael Lee (2/25/2008)

❏ 82. It's Your Ship: Management Techniques from the Best Damn Ship in the Navy
Abrashoff, Capt. D. Michael (3/31/2008)

❏ 96. *The Prince of Darkness: 50 Years Reporting in Washington
Novak, Robert D. (7/14/2008) `Top-10 Book`

❏ 98. LeaderShift: Letting Go of Leadership Heresies
Cousins, Don (7/29/2008)

❏ 110. The Truth About Managing People and Nothing But the Truth
Robbins, Stephen P. (10/20/2008)

❏ 111. Margin: Restoring Emotional, Physical, Financial and Time Reserves to Overloaded Lives
Swenson M.D., Richard A. (10/27/2008)

❏ 122. *Strengths Based Leadership: Great Leaders, Teams and Why People Follow
Rath, Tom and Conchie, Barry (1/12/2009) `Top-10 Book`

❏ 124. Not Quite What I was Planning: Six-Word Memoirs by Writers Famous and Obscure
Fershleiser, Rachel and Smith, Larry (editors) (1/27/2009)

❏ 138. Leadership RE:Vision - Looking at Leadership With a New Set of Eyes
Seybert, Jim (5/6/2009)

❏ 145. Transforming Together: Authentic Spiritual Mentoring
Parrott, Ele (6/25/2009)

❏ 156. Bo's Café: A Novel
Lynch, Bill; Thrall, Bill and McNicol, Bruce (9/25/2009)

☐ 161. The Joseph Road: Choices That Determine Your Destiny
White, Jerry (10/31/2009)

▶2009 Book-of-the-Year
☐ 168 & 181. *Strengthening the Soul of Your Leadership: Seeking God in the Crucible of Ministry
Barton, Ruth Haley (12/23/2009, 4/17/2010) Book-of-the-Year

▶2010 Book-of-the-Year
☐ 191 & 328. *The First 90 Days: Critical Success Factors for New Leaders at All Levels
Watkins, Michael (7/23/2010) Top-10 Book

☐ 194. King Vidor's Our Daily Bread (DVD)
Vidor, King (Director) - (8/24/2010)

☐ 209. *The Talent Masters: Why Smart Leaders Put People Before Numbers
Conaty, Bill and Charan, Ram (2/22/2011) Top-10 Book

☐ 223. Managing Your Boss (*Harvard Business Review* article)
Gabarro, John J. and Kotter, John P. (7/14/2011)

☐ 231. The Gift of Rest: Rediscovering the Beauty of the Sabbath
Lieberman, Joe (9/22/2011)

☐ 238. *The Cure: What If God Isn't Who You Think He Is and Neither Are You
Lynch, John; McNicol, Bruce and Thrall, Bill (12/23/2011) Top-10 Book

☐ 241. *Eat That Frog! 21 Great Ways to Stop Procrastinating and Get More Done in Less Time
Tracy, Brian (1/19/2012) Top-10 Book

☐ 250. Heroes: From Alexander the Great and Julius Caesar to Churchill and De Gaulle
Johnson, Paul (5/31/2012)

☐ 264. First Aid for Enablers: Ten Treatments for Enablers and the Addicts They Love
Curry, David (12/24/2012)

☐ 267. I've Got Your Back: A Leadership Parable — Biblical Principles for Leading and Following Well
Galvin, James C. (1/22/2013) Top-10 Book

☐ 233A. What You Do Best in the Body of Christ: Discover Your Spiritual Gifts, Personal Style and God-Given Passion - Bugbee, Bruce (10/13/2011)

☐ 233B. Discover Your Spiritual Gifts: The Easy-to-Use Guide That Helps You Identify and Understand Your God-Given Spiritual Gifts - Wagner, C. Peter (10/13/2011)

☐ 296. To Be a Friend: Building Deep and Lasting Relationships
by Jerry and Mary White (4/9/2014) Top-10 Book

☐ 303C. Managing for Dummies®
Bob Nelson and Peter Economy (7/12/2014)

☐ 309. Entrepreneurial StrengthsFinder
by Jim Clifton and Sangeeta Bharadwaj Badal, Ph.D. (10/17/2014) Top-10 Book

❏ 313. The Boys in the Boat: Nine Americans and Their Epic Quest for Gold at the 1936 Berlin Olympics by Daniel James Brown (11/29/14) `Top-10 Book`

❏ 320. Great Questions for Leading Well, by Steve Brown (3/20/15)

❏ 322. Leaders Eat Last: Why Some Teams Pull Together and Others Don't, by Simon Sinek (4/8/15) `Top-10 Book`

❏ 328. The First 90 Days: Critical Success Factors for New Leaders at All Levels Watkins, Michael (rerun: 7/7/15 - See Issue 191, 7/23/2010) `Top-10 Book`

❏ 329. Connection Culture: The Competitive Advantage of Shared Identity, Empathy, and Understanding at Work, by Michael Lee Stallard, Jason Pankau, and Katharine P. Stallard (7/29/15) `Top-10 Book`

❏ 337B. Listen to My Life: Maps for Recognizing and Responding to God in My Story by Sibyl Towner and Sharon Swing (1/20/16)

❏ 338. The Coaching Habit: Say Less, Ask More & Change the Way You Lead Forever by Michael Bungay Stanier, (1/27/16) `Top-10 Book`

❏ 339. Leading Me: Eight Practices for a Christian Leader's Most Important Assignment by Steve A. Brown (3/5/16) `Top-10 Book`

❏ 344. The Ideal Team Player: How to Recognize and Cultivate the Three Essential Virtues by Patrick Lencioni (6/20/16) `Top-10 Book`

❏ 349B. [Video]: "Everybody Needs a Coach" (StrengthsFinder) by The Gallup Organization (9/1/16)

❏ 358. Make Your Bed: Little Things That Can Change Your Life...and Maybe the World Admiral William H. McRaven (U.S. Navy Retired) (4/22/17)

❏ 360. Overcoming Conflict: How to Deal with Difficult People and Situations Bob Phillips (5/20/17)

Author: Ralph E. Enlow, Jr.

Arresting PowerPoint slides jump off almost every page:

☑ "You can't make up in training what you lack in selection."

☑ "Leaders ignore culture at their peril."

☑ "The responsibility of every godly leader is to resist the subtle temptations to convert their credibility into celebrity."

#10. The *Hoopla!* Bucket (By Issue Number and Book Review Date)

❒ 36. The Carrot Principle: How the Best Managers Use Recognition to Engage Their People, Retain Talent, and Accelerate Performance - Gostick, Adrian and Elton, Chester (5/7/2007)

❒ 129. Monday Morning Leadership: 8 Mentoring Sessions You Can't Afford to Miss
Cottrell, David (3/3/2009)

❒ 180. In Search of Excellence: Lessons from America's Best-Run Companies
Peters, Thomas J. & Waterman, Robert H. (4/11/2010)

❒ 294. A Nice Little Place on the North Side: Wrigley Field at One Hundred
by George F. Will (3/3/2014)

❒ 321. Humorists: From Hogarth to Noel Coward,
by Paul Johnson (4/1/2015)

❒ 364. The Cubs Way: The Zen of Building the Best Team in Baseball and Breaking the Curse
Tom Verducci (7/13/17) `Top-10 Book`

▶**2017 Book-of-the-Year**
❒ 372. The Power of Moments: Why Certain Experiences Have Extraordinary Impact
Chip Heath and Dan Heath (11/25/17)

#11. The Donor Bucket (By Issue Number and Book Review Date)

❒ 10. 40 Day Spiritual Journey to a More Generous Life
Kluth, Brian (10/30/2006)

❒ 14. Major Donor Game Plan: Rounding 3rd and Heading Home
McLaughlin, Patrick (11/27/2006)

❒ 26. The Treasure Principle: Unlocking the Secret of Joyful Giving
Alcorn, Randy (2/26/2007)

❒ 35. The 7 Deadly Sins of Christian Fundraising
Rodin, R. Scott (4/30/2007)

❒ 89. *Revolution in Generosity: Transforming Stewards to Be Rich Toward God
Willmer, Wesley K (general editor)   (5/19/2008) `Top-10 Book`

❒ 104. Made to Stick: Why Some Ideas Survive and Others Die
Heath, Chip (9/8/2008)

❒ 113. The One Year Mini for Leaders
Seybert, Jim (11/10/2008)

❏ 125. Passing the Plate: Why American Christians Don't Give Away More Money
Emerson, Michael O. and Snell, Patricia (2/2/2009)

❏ 128. The Giving Journey: A Guide to the Joy of Generosity
MacDonald, Gordon and Johnson, Patrick (2/24/2009)

❏ 134. *The Hole in Our Gospel: What Does God Expect of Us? The Answer That Changed My Life and Might Just Change the World - Stearns, Richard (4/6/2009) `Top-10 Book`

❏ 157. The Hole in Our Gospel: Personal Action Journal
CrossSection (9/30/2009)

❏ 166. Being Generous
Malloch, Theodore Roosevelt (12/4/2009)

❏ 171. Spiritual Enterprise: Doing Virtuous Business
Malloch, Theodore Roosevelt (1/20/2010)

❏ 197. *The Sower: Redefining the Ministry of Raising Kingdom Resources
Rodin, R. Scott and Hoag, Gary G. (9/27/2010) `Top-10 Book`

❏ 218. *The Third Conversion
Rodin, R. Scott (5/19/2011) `Top-10 Book`

❏ 234. Igniting a Life of Generosity
McDaniel, Chris (10/24/2011)

❏ 248. *The Million-Dollar Dime (A Novelette)
Rodin, R. Scott (5/9/2012) `Top-10 Book`

❏ 263. Giving & Getting in the Kingdom: A Field Guide
Dillon, R. Mark (12/15/2012)

❏ 287. Stewardship as a Lifestyle: Seeking to Live as a Steward and Disciple
Frank, John R. (10/18/2013)

❏ 327A. Development 101: Building a Comprehensive Development Program on Biblical Values,
by John Frank and R. Scott Rodin (6/23/15)

❏ 327B. Ignite Your Generosity: A 21-Day Experience in Stewardship,
by Chris McDaniel (6/23/15) - (Note: revised and published by IVP in 2015)

❏ 340B. The Guide to Charitable Giving for Churches and Ministries
By Dan Busby, Michael Martin, and John Van Drunen (3/21/16)

❏ 353A. The Seventh Key: Unlocking the Life God Created You to Live (A Novelette)
by R. Scott Rodin (12/23/16) `Top-10 Book`

#12. The Volunteer Bucket (By Issue Number and Book Review Date)

❏ 34. Halftime: Changing Your Game Plan From Success to Significance
Buford, Bob (4/23/2007)

❏ 60. Forces for Good: The Six Practices of High-Impact Nonprofits
Crutchfield, Leslie R. and Grant, Heather McLeod (10/29/2007)

❏ 83B. Simply Strategic Volunteers: Empowering People for Ministry
Morgan, Tony and Stevens, Tim (4/7/2008)

❏ 361. The Gatekeepers: How the White House Chiefs of Staff Define Every Presidency, by Chris Whipple
(Part 1 of 2: 6/14/17)

❏ 362. The Gatekeepers: How the White House Chiefs of Staff Define Every Presidency (Part 2 of 2), by
Chris Whipple (Part 2 of 2: 6/21/17)

#13. The Crisis Bucket (By Issue Number and Book Review Date)

❏ 78. Judgment: How Winning Leaders Make Great Calls
Tichy, Noel M. and Bennis, Warren G. (3/3/2008)

❏ 137. The Noticer: Sometimes, All a Person Needs Is a Little Perspective
Andrews, Andy (4/27/2009)

❏ 155. Fearless: Imagine Your Life Without Fear
Lucado, Max (9/14/2009)

❏ 221. Eisenhower 1956: The President's Year of Crisis—Suez and the Brink of War
Nichols, David A. (6/30/2011)

❏ 252. *The Presidents Club: Inside the World's Most Exclusive Fraternity
Gibbs, Nancy and Duff, Michael (7/5/2012) `Top-10 Book`

❏ 348. 100 Deadly Skills: The SEAL Operative's Guide to Eluding Pursuers, Evading Capture, and
Surviving Any Dangerous Situation
by Clint Emerson, Navy SEAL, Ret. (8/27/16)

George H.W. Bush upon losing the election to Bill Clinton:

"…at five the next morning [Bush] got out his list of several hundred people he needed to thank and reached for the phone. He got off sixteen hours later."

THE CORPORATION
To read a book review (and order the book), click on "Archives" at
www.urgentink.typepad.com
or Google "[the book title], John Pearson's Buckets Blog"

Top-10 Book = Named one of the "Top-10 Books" reviewed in that year by John Pearson (effective 2008).
▶**Book-of-the-Year**= Named "Book-of-the-Year" by John Pearson (effective 2008).
The 2018 honors will be announced December 31, 2018 in *Your Weekly Staff Meeting* eNews.

#14. The Board Bucket (By Issue Number and Book Review Date)

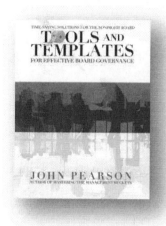

New at Amazon!

Tools and Templates for Effective Board Governance: Time-Saving Solutions for the Nonprofit Board, by John Pearson

"…full of practical, helpful tools to assist in the development of excellent board governance."
Patrick C. Clements

❒ 11. The Imperfect Board Member: Discovering the Seven Disciplines of Governance Excellence
Brown, Jim (11/6/2006)

❒ 28. Nonprofit Board Answer Book
Andringa, Robert and Engstrom, Ted (3/12/2007)

❒ 50. Good Governance for Nonprofits: Developing Principles and Policies for an Effective Board
Laughlin, Frederic L. and Andringa, Robert C. (8/20/2007)

❒ 58. Nonprofit Board Answer Book: A Practical Guide for Board Members and Chief Executives (Second Edition) – BoardSource (10/15/2007)

❒ 88. The Perfect Search: What Every Nonprofit Board Member Needs to Know About Hiring Their Next CEO - Thomas, Tommy with Isbister, Nick and Andringa, Robert C. (5/12/2008)

❒ 123. The Leader's Legacy
McKenna, David L. (1/20/2009)

❒ 170 *Owning Up: The 14 Questions Every Board Member Needs to Ask
Charan, Ram (1/11/2010) **Top-10 Book**

❒ 198. Governance as Leadership: Reframing the Work of Nonprofit Boards
Chait, Richard P.; Ryan, William P. and Taylor, Barbara E. (10/9/2010)

❏ 207. Stewards of a Sacred Trust: CEO Selection, Transition and Development for Boards of Christ-centered Organizations - McKenna, David L. (1/28/2011)

❏ 212. The Hero's Farewell: What Happens When CEOs Retire
Sonnenfeld, Jeffrey (3/22/2011)

❏ 226. Boards That Make a Difference: A New Design for Leadership in Nonprofit Organizations
Carver, John (8/12/2011)

❏ 240. Boost! 52 Infusions of Wisdom to Revolutionize the Way You Think and Live.
Curry, Dean (1/6/2012)

❏ 249. The Nonprofit Board Answer Book: A Practical Guide for Board Members and Chief Executives (3rd Edition) BoardSource (5/22/2012)

❏ 253. Board Member Orientation: The Concise and Complete Guide to Nonprofit Board Service
Batts, Michael E. (7/12/2012)

❏ 260. *ECFA Governance Toolbox Series No. 1: Recruiting Board Members (DVD, Viewing Guide & Facilitator Guide) - ECFA (10/30/2012) `Top-10 Book`

❏ 244. What Makes Great Boards Great (*Harvard Business Review* article)
Sonnenfeld, Jeffrey (3/15/2012)

❏ 276. ECFA Governance Toolbox Series No. 2: Balancing Board Roles – Understanding the 3 Board Hats: Governance, Volunteer, Participant (DVD, Viewing Guide & Facilitator Guide) – ECFA (5/8/2013) `Top-10 Book`

❏ 284. Policy vs. Paper Clips: How Using the Corporate Model Makes a Nonprofit Board More Efficient & Effective (3rd Edition)
Fram, Eugene H. with Brown, Vicki (8/27/2013)

❏ 295. Boards That Lead: When to Take Charge, When to Partner, and When to Stay Out of the Way
by Ram Charan, Dennis Carey and Michael Useem (3/28/2014) `Top-10 Book`

❏ 311A. Serving as a Board Member: Practical Guidance for Directors of Christian Ministries
by John Pellowe (11/6/14)

❏ 311B. Best Practices for Effective Boards
by E. LeBron Fairbanks, Dwight M. Gunter II, and James R. Cauchenour (11/6/14)

❏ 311C. Board Essentials: 12 Best Practices of Nonprofit Boards
by David L. Coleman (11/6/14)

❏ 311D. Ten Basic Responsibilities of Nonprofit Boards (Second Edition)
by Richard T. Ingram (11/6/14)

❏ 311E. ECFA 3rd Annual Nonprofit Governance Survey
Published by ECFA (11/6/14)

❏ 325A. ECFA Governance Toolbox Series No. 3: Addressing Board and Organizational Conflicts of Interest—Avoiding Trouble, Trouble, Trouble With Related–Party Transactions
Published by ECFA (5/13/15)

❐ 325B. The Invisible Gorilla: And Other Ways Our Intuitions Deceive Us,
by Christopher F. Chabris and Daniel Dimons (5/13/15)

❐ 352A. Called to Serve: Creating and Nurturing the Effective Volunteer Board
by Max De Pree 12/7/16) `Top-10 Book`
  ➔**Follow John Pearson's 30-blog series from the book at:**
     http://ecfagovernance.blogspot.com/2017/10/called-to-serve-no-board-detail-is-too.html

❐ 352B. Going for Impact: The Nonprofit Director's Essential Guidebook
by Eugene H. Fram with Vicki Brown (12/7/16)

❐ 363. Call of the Chair: Leading the Board of the Christ-centered Ministry
David L. McKenna (6/28/17) `Top-10 Book`

The latest addition to the Board Bucket:

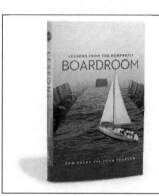

Hot-off-the-Press: November 2017!

❐ 373. Lessons From the Nonprofit Boardroom
Dan Busby and John Pearson (11/20/17) `Top-10 Book`

Follow 40 guest bloggers for "40 Blogs. 40 Wednesdays."
http://nonprofitboardroom.blogspot.com/

Order at Amazon:
http://amzn.to/2Eo1Zrx

#15. The Budget Bucket (By Issue Number and Book Review Date)

❐ 9. The Minister's MBA: Essential Business Tools for Maximum Ministry Success
Babbes, George S. and Zigarelli, Michael (10/23/2006)

❐ 83. Cents & Sensibility: How Couples Can Agree About Money
Palmer, Scott and Bethany (4/7/2008)

❐ 91. Zone of Insolvency: How Nonprofits Avoid Hidden Liabilities and Build Financial Strength
Mattocks, Ron (6/2/2008)

❐ 106. The Best Investment Advice I Ever Received
Claman, Liz (9/22/2008)

❐ 131. First Comes Love, Then Comes Money: A Couple's Guide to Financial Communication
Palmer, Scott and Bethany (3/17/2009)

❐ 266A. Zondervan 2013 Church and Nonprofit Tax & Financial Guide
Busby, Dan; Martin, J. Michael and Van Drunen, John (1/16/2013)

❐ 266B. Zondervan 2013 Minister's Tax & Financial Guide
Busby, Dan; Martin, J. Michael and Van Drunen, John (1/16/2013)

❒ 293A. Zondervan 2014 Minister's Tax & Financial Guide (for 2013 returns), by Dan Busby, CPA, J. Michael Martin, JD, and John Van Drunen, JD, CPA

❒ 293B. Zondervan 2014 Church and Nonprofit Tax & Financial Guide (for 2013 returns) by Dan Busby, CPA, J. Michael Martin, JD, and John Van Drunen, JD, CPA

❒ 293C. The 5 Money Personalities: Speaking the Same Love and Money Language by Scott and Bethany Palmer

❒ 317A. Zondervan 2015 Minister's Tax & Financial Guide (for 2014 returns), by Dan Busby, CPA, J. Michael Martin, JD, and John Van Drunen, JD, CPA (2/4/15)

❒ 317B. Zondervan 2015 Church and Nonprofit Tax & Financial Guide (for 2014 returns) by Dan Busby, CPA, J. Michael Martin, JD, and John Van Drunen, JD, CPA (2/4/15)

❒ 317C. The 5 Money Conversations to Have With Your Kids at Every Age and Stage, by Scott and Bethany Palmer (2/4/15)

❒ 331B. ECFA Nonprofit Financial Management Survey 1.0, published by ECFA (10/14/15)
➔ download at http://www.ecfa.org/content/surveys

❒ 340C. Zondervan 2016 Church and Nonprofit Tax & Financial Guide for 2015 Returns By Dan Busby, Michael Martin, and John Van Drunen (3/21/16)

❒ 340D. Zondervan 2016 Minister's Tax & Financial Guide for 2015 Returns By Dan Busby, Michael Martin, and John Van Drunen (3/21/16)

❒ 355A. Zondervan 2017 Church and Nonprofit Tax & Financial Guide for 2016 Returns By Dan Busby, Michael Martin, and John Van Drunen (2/3/17)

❒ 355B. Zondervan 2017 Minister's Tax & Financial Guide for 2016 Returns By Dan Busby, Michael Martin, and John Van Drunen (2/3/17)

❒ 355C. Jesus' Terrible Financial Advice: Flipping the Tables on Peace, Prosperity, and the Pursuit of Happiness, by John Thornton (2/3/17)

❒ 374. The God Guarantee: Finding Freedom From the Fear of Not Having Enough Jack Alexander (12/6/17)

#16. The Delegation Bucket (By Issue Number and Book Review Date)

❒ 7. Joy at Work: A Revolutionary Approach to Fun on the Job Bakke, Dennis (10/9/2006)

❒ 12. The One Minute Manager Meets the Monkey Blanchard, Ken and Oncken Jr., William (11/13/2006)

❒ 119. Mastering the Management Buckets: 20 Critical Competencies for Leading Your Business or Nonprofit - Pearson, John (12/22/2008)

❏ 153. Spiritual Leadership: Principles of Excellence for Every Believer
Sanders, J. Oswald (8/26/2009)

❏ 202. A Message to Garcia
Hubbard, Elbert (11/24/2010)

❏ 272. The Decision Maker: Unlock the Potential of Everyone in Your Organization One Decision at a Time
Bakke, Dennis (3/28/2013) `Top-10 Book`

❏ 273. How to Delegate (CD, 39 min.)
Mackenzie, Alec (4/2/2013)

❏ 356A. Time Management Made (Stupidly) Easy: A Modestly Simple Guide to Time Management
Michael R. Clarke (3/2/17)

❏ 356B (reminder!). How to Delegate (CD, 39 min.)
Mackenzie, Alec (4/2/2013)

❏ 366. Top Ten Ways to Be a Great Leader, by Hans Finzel (8/18/17)

#17. The Operations Bucket (By Issue Number and Book Review Date)

❏ 21. The Starfish and the Spider: The Unstoppable Power of Leaderless Organizations
Brafman, Ori and Beckstrom, Rod A. (1/22/2007)

❏ 38. If You Haven't Got the Time to Do It Right…When Will You Find the Time to Do It Over?
Mayer, Jeffrey J. (5/21/2007)

❏ 43. The Unnatural Act of Management: When the Great Leader's Work Is Done, the People Say "We Did It Ourselves" - Suters, Everett T. (6/25/2007)

❏ 59. Wikinomics: How Mass Collaboration Changes Everything
Tapscott, Don and Williams, Anthony D. (10/22/2007)

❏ 64. Managing Transitions: Making the Most of Change
Bridges, William (11/26/2007)

❏ 114. The Essential Engstrom: Proven Principles of Leadership
Engstrom, Ted W. (11/17/2008)

❏ 152. Success Scenarios (24 core professional skills training sessions)
Russell, David (8/19/2009)

❏ 195. *Operation Mincemeat: How a Dead Man and a Bizarre Plan Fooled the Nazis and Assured an Allied Victory - Macintyre, Ben (9/7/2010) `Top-10 Book`

❏ 230. The 7 Habits of Highly Effective People
by Stephen R. Covey (9/12/2011)

❏ 347. Be the Director I Could Follow
by Earl D. Taylor (8/3/16)

Outrageous, by Aaron Tredway

LOOK UP! Do you tilt toward anonymity—head down, To-Do list imperatives, yet perhaps miss the people God has put in your path? Look up and read Chapter 6, "Ben's Bunnies," (hilarious!) and don't miss Tredway's quote from Os Guinness (the great-great-great-grandson of the brewer):

"Our problem is not that we aren't where we should be, but that we aren't what we should be where we are."

#18. The Systems Bucket (By Issue Number and Book Review Date)

❐ 32. The E-Myth Revisited: Why Most Small Businesses Don't Work and What to Do About It
Gerber, Michael E. (4/9/2007)

❐ 40. The Organized Executive: The Classic Program for Productivity--New Ways to Manage Time, Paper, People and the Digital Office - Winston, Stephanie (6/4/2007)

❐ 117. *Getting Things Done: The Art of Stress-Free Productivity
Allen, David (12/8/2008) `Top-10 Book`

❐ 162. You're Not the Person I Hired! A CEO's Survival Guide to Hiring Top Talent
Boydell, Janet; Deutsch, Barry and Remillard, Brad (11/7/2009)

❐ 173. *The Checklist Manifesto: How to Get Things Right
Gawande, Atul (2/8/2010) `Top-10 Book`

❐ 211. Poke the Box: When Was the Last Time You Did Something for the First Time?
Godin, Seth (3/12/2011)

❐ 227 & 228. *Smart Moves for People in Charge: 130 Checklists to Help You Be a Better Leader
Deep, Sam and Sussman, Lyle (8/20/2011) `Top-10 Book`

❐ 285. Manage Your Day-to-Day: Build Your Routine, Find Your Focus, and Sharpen Your Creative Mind
Glei, Jocelyn K., Editor (9/9/2013) `Top-10 Book`

❐ 349A. Systems Church IT: Strategies and Solutions
by Nick B. Nicholaou (9/1/16)

❐ 356. Time Management Made (Stupidly) Easy: A Modestly Simple Guide to Time Management, by Michael R. Clarke (3/2/17)

❐ 365. Leading the Other Way: How to Change the Church Planting World,
by JD Pearring

❐ 371. Growing Weeders Into Leaders: Leadership Lessons from the Ground Level
Jeff McManus (10/17/17) `Top-10 Book`

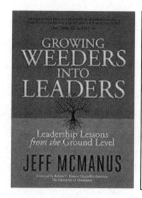

WHAT'S WORSE? PowerPoint-worthy quotes on almost every page will juice your coaching competencies, like this one from John Maxwell: **"What's worse than training your people and losing them? Not training them and keeping them."**

#19. The Printing Bucket (By Issue Number and Book Review Date)
aka: The Communication Bucket, The Speaking Bucket, etc.

❐ 27. How to Get Your Point Across in 30 Seconds--or Less
Frank, Milo O. (3/5/2007)

❐ 109. *You've Got to Be Believed to Be Heard: The Complete Book of Speaking in Business and in Life
Decker, Bert (10/14/2008) `Top-10 Book`

❐ 130. Barack, Inc. - Winning Business Lessons of the Obama Campaign
Libert, Barry and Faulk, Rick (3/10/2009)

❐ 176. The Best of Success: A Treasury of Inspiration
Anderson, Mac & Kelly, Bob (3/9/2010)

❐ 200. Keys to Great Writing
Wilbers, Stephen (10/27/2010)

❐ 214. Waiting for "Superman" (DVD)
Guggenheim, David (Director) - (4/14/2011)

❐ 216. *15 Minutes Including Q&A: A Plan to Save the World From Lousy Presentations
Asher, Joey (5/4/2011) `Top-10 Book`

❐ 222. Hitler in the Crosshairs: A GI's Story of Courage and Faith
Woodbridge, John and Possley, Maurice (7/8/2011)

❐ 256. *How to Deliver a TED Talk: Secrets of the World's Most Inspiring Presentations
Donovan, Jeremey (9/5/2012) `Top-10 Book`

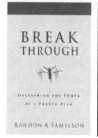

Randy Samelson:

Answer this brilliant question in 15 words or less (his rules!):

KEY LOG QUESTION: "Other than money, what one opportunity (or obstacle) if captured (or removed) would most advance your mission/vision?"

#20. The Meetings Bucket (By Issue Number and Book Review Date)

❒ 84. Leadership Gold: Lessons I've Learned From a Lifetime of Leading - Maxwell, John C. (4/14/2008)

❒ 102. Beyond Bullet Points: Using Microsoft Office PowerPoint 2007 to Create Presentations That Inform, Motivate and Inspire - Atkinson, Cliff (8/25/2008)

❒ 103. The Bucket List (DVD) - Reiner, Rob (Director) - (9/1/2008)

❒ 146. The Hamster Revolution for Meetings: How to Meet Less and Get More Done
Halsey, Vicki and Burress, Tim (6/30/2009)

❒ 236. Death by Meeting: A Leadership Fable…About Solving the Most Painful Problem in Business
Lencioni, Patrick (12/2/2011)

❒ 259. Read This Before Our Next Meeting: The Modern Meeting Standard for Successful Organizations
Pittampalli, Al (10/19/2012)

❒ 308. Unbroken: A World War II Story of Survival, Resilience, and Redemption
by Laura Hillenbrand (10/2/2014—Read the review to see why it's in the "Meetings Bucket" category) **Top-10 Book**

❒ 367. The Secret to a Good Meeting Is the Meeting Before the Meeting: Lesson 18 from Leadership Gold (Kindle Edition), by John C. Maxwell (8/30/17)

"The Bonus Bucket" (By Issue Number and Book Review Date) – 11 Mini-Reviews

			LAST-MINUTE GIFT BUYING OPTIONS FOR YOUR TEAM MEMBERS, FRIENDS AND FAMILY: Mini-Reviews	
375A	12/22/17	Results	Don't Step in the Leadership: A Dilbert Book by Scott Adams	Scott Adams
375B	12/22/17	Operations	The Leadership Secrets of Santa: How to Get Big Things Done in YOUR "Workshop"…All Year Long	Eric Harvey, David Cottrell, Al Lucia, and Mike Hourigan
375C	12/22/17	People	Don't Let Jerks Get the Best of You: Advice for Dealing With Difficult People	Paul Meier, M.D.
375D	12/22/17	Strategy	Breakthrough the Ick Factors of Nonprofit Leadership: Discover Your Organization's True Potential	Tom Okarma
375E	12/22/17	Hoopla!	The Big Ideas Notepad: 100 Brainstorming, Mind-Mapping & Awesome Idea-Generating Sheets	Mary Kate McDevitt (Artist)
375F	12/22/17	Hoopla!	Amazon Gift Card (Invest in books for your team members!)	Amazon
375G	12/22/17	Strategy	Change Is Good…You Go First: 21 Ways to Inspire Change	Max Anderson and Tom Feltenstein
375H	12/22/17	Book	How Much Land Does A Man Need (Classics To Go) – Kindle Book	Leo Tolstoy
375I	12/22/17	Team	The Leadership Secrets of Billy Graham	Harold Myra and Marshall Shelley
375J	12/22/17	Book	Raising Your Kids to Love the Lord	Dave Stone
375K	12/22/17	Hoopla!	Cartoons from The New Yorker: 2018 Day-to-Day Calendar	New Yorker Magazine
376	12/22/17	Book	***TOP 10 BOOKS FOR 2017 & BOOK OF THE YEAR**	

Leaders Are Readers (and Listeners!): Delegate Your Reading!

❑ Each month, give your direct reports one book to read.

❑ Ask for a 5- to 10-minute "book review" from one person each week.

❑ Your team will be inspired, motivated and will learn something
from reading 4 books x 11 months = 44 books per year!

❑ Then…file the book on your staff resource shelf with your marked-up copies so your managers can mentor their people with niche chapters.

❑ For more ideas, see the Book Bucket chapter in *Mastering the Management Buckets*, by John Pearson, or visit: http://managementbuckets.com/book-bucket

Visit www.managementbuckets.com/book-bucket
for the **Master List** of all book reviews,
segmented into the 20 Management Buckets categories.

BOARD GOVERNANCE &
MANAGEMENT CONSULTANTS
FOR
NONPROFIT MINISTRIES,
CHURCHES,
& ASSOCIATIONS

JOHNPEARSONASSOCIATES

JOHN PEARSON ASSOCIATES, INC.
P.O. Box 74985
San Clemente, CA 92673
Mobile: 949.500.0334
John@JohnPearsonAssociates.com

BLOGS & WEBSITES

Books: www.urgentink.typepad.com
Boards: www.ecfagovernance.blogspot.com
Boardrooms: www.nonprofitboardroom.blogspot.com
Buckets: www.ManagementBuckets.com

"My best friend is a person who will give me a book I have not read."
Abraham Lincoln

BOOKS AND WORKBOOKS BY JOHN PEARSON
Purchase at Amazon.com

1990 **Marketing Your Ministry: Ten Critical Principles** John Pearson and Robert D. Hisrich, Ph.D.	**2008** **Mastering the Management Buckets** John Pearson	**2017** **Mastering the Management Buckets Workbook** **(2nd Edition, 2018)** John Pearson	**2017** **Lessons From the Nonprofit Boardroom** Dan Busby and John Pearson

NEW in 2018!

Tools and Templates for Effective Board Governance: *Time-Saving Solutions for the Nonprofit Board*
John Pearson

COMING FALL 2018!

Lessons From the Church Boardroom
Dan Busby and John Pearson

☑Yes!

I would like to receive your
complimentary eNewsletter.

Subscribe online at http://managementbuckets.com/enews

"Vision without execution
is delusion"

PETER DRUCKER

JOHNPEARSONASSOCIATES

P.O. Box 74985
San Clemente, CA 92673
Mobile: 949.500.0334
John@JohnPearsonAssociates.com

Your Weekly Staff Meeting is emailed free one to three times a month to subscribers,
the frequency of which is based on an algorithm of
book length, frequent flyer miles, and client deadlines.

ABOUT THE AUTHORS

JOHN PEARSON is a board governance and management consultant from San Clemente, California, and author of *Mastering the Management Buckets: 20 Critical Competencies for Leading Your Business or Nonprofit.* John is co-author with Dan Busby of *Lessons From the Nonprofit Boardroom* (November 2017) and *Lessons from the Church Boardroom* (Sept. 2018).

John served 30 years as a nonprofit ministry CEO, including 25 years as CEO of Christian Camp and Conference Association, Willow Creek Association, and Christian Management Association (now Christian Leadership Alliance).

He is the editor and publisher of *Your Weekly Staff Meeting eNews*—with more than 400 reviews of leadership, management, and governance books.

For fun (and sometimes work) John, and his wife, Joanne, have traveled to over 50 countries.

Websites, Blogs, and Book Reviews:
❑ www.managementbuckets.com/about
❑ www.ecfagovernance.blogspot.com/
❑ www.nonprofitboardroom.blogspot.com/
❑ www.urgentink.typepad.com/

Color Commentary by:

Websites:
www.pearpod.com
www.JasonPearson.com

JASON PEARSON's unique firm, PEARPOD, leverages branding, digital, print and video tools to create unexpected outcomes for nonprofit and for-profit clients. Based in San Clemente, California, Jason began his career in New York City as the co-founder of *Blender Magazine.* He has received numerous artistic awards and his work has been published in more than 30 books. *New York Magazine* recognized Pearson as one of their "digital visionaries." He was also named to the Samsung Brain Trust. With paintings shown in Chicago, San Francisco, Kansas City, and New York, Pearson's work is also featured in the permanent collections of the Smithsonian and Victoria and Albert Museum. He is the author of *10 Admissions: Coloring Book + Ministry Storytelling Manual,* and other books and resources. Jason and his wife, Melinda, homeschool their five children, including triplet teenagers.

Made in the USA
San Bernardino, CA
16 July 2019